Choose Connection

THE PATH TOWARD AUTHENTIC PERSONAL,
PROFESSIONAL, AND SPIRITUAL TRANSFORMATION

DAVID GIULIANO

Published by
Without Boundaries Coaching
4721 Laurel Canyon Boulevard, Suite 200
Studio City, California 91607

© 2015 David Giuliano
All rights reserved
Printed and bound in the United States
11 10 09 08 4 3 2 1
First Edition

Ordering information:
Special discounts are available on quantity purchases by corporations, associations, and other groups. For complete information, contact Without Boundaries Coaching: Tel. (818) 540-6253 or www.withoutboundariescoaching.com.

Publisher's Cataloging-in-Publication data
Giuliano, David. Choose Connection: The path toward authentic personal, professional and spiritual transformation / by David Giuliano.
232 pp. 1.5 cm. ISBN-13: 978-0692520444
1. Nonfiction — Self-help — Personal Transformation. 2. Health, Fitness & Dieting — Mental Health — Happiness. 3. Business & Money — Entrepreneurship & Small Business — Success. I. Giuliano David. II. Choose Connection: The path toward authentic personal, professional and spiritual transformation

Contents

Introduction

This book is the result of a great quest for connection, a deeper relationship with everything that has meaning.

I'm a business and personal coach. When I reflect on my experiences, both personal and professional, I notice a pattern: Where real connection exists, it's possible to achieve great things, but when connection is not present, even what looks like success feels empty, because nothing authentic happens. Nothing genuinely resonates with, expresses, or satisfies the people involved.

My objective in writing this book is to teach you how to be present in your own life, and to show you what's possible if you learn to make real connection—face-to-face, eye-to-eye, heart-to-heart—with everything and everyone you encounter as you follow your own quest toward what means the most to you.

As I work with clients and listen to friends, I hear a whole range of worries and problems:

- "Suddenly, I'm not taking in the kind of money I want to be, and I don't know how to turn things around."

- "I'm good at what I do, but I feel stuck. I need a new way to see my next steps."

- "What's with the women I meet?/What's with my husband?/Why is it so hard to give my family what it needs without giving up on what I need?"

- "I don't know what happened, but my kids seem to be out of control, and I think they see me more as a cash machine than a parent. I don't know how to reach them anymore."

The people who share these concerns with me often have very smooth surfaces—they look competent and successful—but on the basic level of everyday interaction and human satisfaction, things are fraying, or even falling apart.

They look up from life's daily grind to discover the love they used to have for their job or partner is fading. In their offices, no one seems to know how to work together. Big dreams dangle perpetually out of reach.

MANY SYMPTOMS, ONE "DISEASE"

At the root of these seemingly unrelated problems is one thing: A bad or broken connection.

When I say connection, I'm talking about a relationship that allows empathy, respect, honesty, enthusiasm and purpose to flow freely between people, among the parts of the self (mind/ego/heart/soul/spirit), or between the self and the larger world. I can assure you that connection is not abstract or touchy-feely. It's purposeful and decisive. When you decide to make a genuine connection with yourself, other people, and the world, you will bring a new level of energy, clarity, and effectiveness to everything you do.

Connection is the first thing I focus on anytime I listen to a client's problem, because choosing connection is the key to mastering the human side of business and the relationship side of life.

Connection starts inside, and it depends on the energy that comes from knowing yourself well—your gifts, talents, and fears as well as your purely quirky preferences—and bringing that authentic self into the world. Once you start moving through the world as the real you, it gets easier and easier to create strong bonds with other people in every setting, soul-nourishing connections that also happen to produce success and surprises and romantic sparks.

As your connection skills grow, you'll find that the problems in your life recede, because when you know how to connect, you can see—and clear—a path toward the people, activities, inspiration, and solutions that have long eluded you. At the same time, *you'll know when to let go of connections that no longer serve you and replace them with those that do.* As you go through the tools and exercises in this book, you will learn to distinguish between situations that can benefit from this method, those that might require the intervention of a professional such as a therapist or coach, and those that it is best to let go of.

TOOLS TO IMPROVE
EVERY KIND OF CONNECTION

In the chapters that follow, I'll give you the tools to detect and repair broken connections. I'll show you how to build strong connections to your authentic self—the self that reflects your soul, your passions, and your purpose in life—and from there to every part of your life.

For many of us, that's the essential set of skills that no one, even our best teachers and mentors, has ever spelled out.

In part one of the book, I'll give you the tools to reach a new level of honesty with yourself about what you want to be doing, and help you translate that into new plans and ways of dealing with people as you pare away what no longer has meaning for you. You'll free up tremendous energy as you go. I'll also teach you an invaluable process for making decisions that lets you deal with the current of emotions that runs beneath the facts, so you're no longer at the mercy of factors you can't see.

Then I'll show you how to apply these skills in a variety of contexts. The second part of the book drills deep into how to use connection to reshape businesses. Its examples come from the world of entrepreneurs and owners of small businesses and professional practices, but the techniques that it lays out can benefit anyone who's trying to work with a team to achieve a common goal. It will transform your idea of what's possible, and how much satisfaction can come from a business.

The final section of the book focuses more personally on matters of the heart and soul. There you'll find techniques for bringing stronger connection into your relationships with your dating partner or spouse, with your children, and with your spirituality. The same tools and principles you learned at the beginning take on new dimensions applied in this way.

How to use this book

To get the most from this book, I suggest that you take a close look at the first two chapters, whose examples and exercises will help you evaluate and tune up your connection to your authentic self. Spend as much time as you need, using the exercises and establishing the practices I describe in the "Tools for the Road" section at the end of chapter 1. Chapter 2 will give you support when you want to share your authentic decision-making with other people.

From there, follow your interests. The decision-making tool in chapter 3 is something that will serve you in every part of your life. It will require a lot of you if you decide to use it, but you'll be rewarded for every bit of time and thought you give it. If you're pressed for time, or feel overwhelmed, I suggest reading through it, and considering even a few of the questions it asks.

The business chapters distill my connection-centered approach to solving the problems that arise in small businesses. They'll be of particular interest if you're a boss or owner, but will also give great insight to any employee.

Dip into the relationship chapters if you're hungry to build more closeness, honesty, and connection into the significant partnerships and relationships in your life. They're meant to inspire you to take a chance on authenticity, and experience the deep bonds it can produce.

My hope is that you'll use this book to develop the basic skills of connection, then keep it on your shelf so it can be a guide and companion the next time you feel a connection in your life growing faint.

MY PROMISE: THE REWARDS OF CONNECTION WILL OUTWEIGH THE EFFORT

This kind of work may require more self-reflection than you're used to. But don't worry if you've been so busy making a living, putting out fires, and trying to make everyone else happy that you've lost sight of what self-reflection feels like, or have drifted far from what you set out to do in life. I'll give you the practical techniques I use every day to help people gain the insights that power up their own systems—their own being—so they can bring more to the problems they're trying to solve and reconnect with a life that has real meaning for them.

We think that material objects will bring us the sense of fulfillment we crave, or that money will. But that's the big lie of our time. We have endless resources and technology for communication, yet we feel more disconnected than ever. Wherever I go I see people hungry for connection. They can't wait to pick up their phones or computers, and clutch them like they can't let go. The question is, why? What's the feeling they're looking for? What's waiting at the other end of that text or email? Why can't they be where they are? And what is it costing them—costing us—when we don't ask, and can't answer, those questions?

This book will help you replace the illusion of connection with the real thing. You may disagree with some of aspects of my approach, and that's okay. If you take even a few of the steps in this book, you'll open and deepen your own understanding of the power of connection.

Many thought seekers talk about choosing your purpose before you are born. I can't say for certain that that's possible, but the evidence of my life says that if I did make a choice, it was to focus on the journey of living and teaching about the opportunities that exist when we learn to connect. Unconsciously that was always the theme of my life, but I didn't become aware of it until I started looking into myself more deeply. The impact of this new understanding has been so profound that it's driven me to share it with you in this book.

Whatever your goals and dreams, as you move toward them, know this: *Authentic connection comes first, and it can only come from within.*

More than any other skill in business, or in life, the ability to connect, and to mend broken connections, is the most transformative. It can change the most "stuck" situations in your life, and free up storehouses of energy, success, happiness, and love.

You can choose connection. In fact, you already have.

PART I

Connection Starts With You

I grew up under the tutelage of my dad who was a quality-control inspector for the Ford Motor Company for almost thirty years. So you might say attention to detail is a part of my DNA. I've been a serious student of connection since I was twelve years old, working in my uncle's car stereo business installing and repairing anything in automotive electronics. We had a systematic process for figuring out why a radio wouldn't work, and a series of questions to ask as we narrowed down possible problems and solutions. While you can't exactly put a life situation on a testing bench to run diagnostics, I've found that you can learn how and where to look at any part of your life that's giving you trouble, and trace the problems on the surface to specific connection problems under the hood.

The chapters in this section will lead you through questions, tests, and experiments you can run to get to the root causes of what's going wrong.

The first questions we'd ask in the shop were the most basic: Is this thing plugged in? Is it connected to the battery? Interestingly, I find that the most important question to ask a client facing any

problem deals with exactly the same issue: How well are you connected to what gives you energy—your own passion and purpose?
That's the personal power source from which everything else
flows. In that authentic core is the current that will fuel your connection to success, satisfying home and family life, and the ability
to build deep, meaningful relationships in the wider world and
even with your own spirituality.

Knowing and doing what you value and enjoy, and being who
you genuinely are, isn't a "someday" goal to think about when
you're retired, or when there's finally less stress in your life. It's the
juice that powers everything.

That's not what most people think will rescue their businesses,
save their relationships, double their incomes, or help them deal
with thorn-in-the-side employees. They're often skeptical about
how focusing on themselves will help anything—until they see the
life-changing results.

I'll show you how to work from the inside out, and give you a
whole array of tools for cutting through stuck or difficult situations
by spotting where, when and how the underlying connections went
bad. I will also show you how to rebuild or discard parts that no
longer work. Just as I used to scan circuit boards for cracks and
damaged transistors, you'll learn to test the integrity of key connections in your life, and pinpoint what's creating static, distortion and
pain.

I'll teach you to look at business challenges, personnel issues,
and home situations as I do, using all your senses to size up what's
really going on, and to develop strategies for making the shifts that
will quickly move you toward the results and relationships you
want. *And I'll encourage you to pay close attention to any tendencies you have
to gloss over the status quo*—"It's been like this forever," or, "I'm used
to it, so I'll assume everything is okay." I learned in my uncle's shop
that you can't assume two wires are properly connected just because they're twisted together. It always pays to bring fresh attention to what's become comfortable, familiar, and (often) invisible.

Whatever your situation—whether you're feeling inspired to
grow your business, desperate to change a stuck situation, hungry

for answers, or challenged by a relationship at home or work—the tools in this section will help you discover what you genuinely want, and tap into the power to create the kind of connection that will pull you toward it.

CHAPTER 1

Bringing Your Authentic Self
Into Your Work Life

In the simple, mechanical world of a car stereo shop, it's obvious that everything needs a power source. You can have the finest components in the world, but without the juice to run them, you've just got expensive junk.

You could say the same of your talents, plans, and desires. They can't come to life without an inner current that pushes them into the world. We often talk about tenacity, motivation, or grit, and believe that to make an idea fly or solve most problems, what we need to do is buckle down, make a plan, and "just do it."

It sounds like simple common sense. But here's the problem: That determined, rational approach draws all its power from intellect and will—in other words, from the mind. And it happens that for the purposes of keeping us connected to what we want to do and improve, the mind, on its own, has all the oomph and staying power of a AAA battery.

Most people don't realize they have been ignoring the equivalent of a 700-horsepower engine that can launch an ambitious dream, drive their growth, and help them move successfully through even the problems that push them toward despair. The real power for creation and change is hidden in the realm of the feelings, specifically feelings like joy, passion, excitement, and love.

I can see the eye rolls from here. Skepticism is common when I walk into a troubled business and start sizing up the situation by asking the principals: "How much do you like what you do?"

The common response, whether it's blurted out or muttered under someone's breath, is, "What's that got to do with the problem?" My answer: Everything.

The same holds true when I talk to people about their stressful relationships. One of the most telling ways to find out what's really going on in a distant marriage or a sticky office personnel problem is to ask each party, "How much do you let yourself do what you really love?"

Think of what happens inside you when you're fully engaged in something, noticing with a quiet kind of awe, "I love this. I was meant to do it. It makes me feel alive." Much depends on how well and how often you bring that energy into your everyday life—your work, your friendships, your dealings with your family. It doesn't matter what gives you that feeling—it can be anything. Your kids, your car, the New York Giants, that crazy idea you have for a side business. *Any* passion will energize you, show you the best of who you are, and remind you of how you most want to be. The passions that give you the electrifying feeling that "I was meant to do this" are your foundation, your compass and your all-important source of power for shaping a satisfying, rewarding life and business. When you know how to stay close to your own desires, dreams and even your goofy enthusiasms—the passions that pull you when you're at your most authentic—you can connect solidly and powerfully to everything else in your life. When you treat the pull of your authentic self as though it's optional or not as important as someone else's priorities, connections to everything else—including that person with the priorities—sputter.

So in this chapter, I'll show you how to check out how well you and your authentic self are connected. As we go, I'll show you examples of what happens when people rediscover the power of making decisions that free up the energy that comes from allowing themselves to be who they are.

In this chapter, we'll look at how reconnecting to the self can transform how you handle work situations. Then, in chapter 2, we'll look at how the same principles, diagnostics and exercises that are so powerful in the workplace can give you new options and effectiveness in non-work relationships.

EIGHT TELLTALE SIGNS THAT IT'S TIME FOR THE JUMPER CABLES IN YOUR BUSINESS LIFE

If you're not solidly connected to your authentic self, you'll see various forms of "static" show up in your work life. The effects, which can be mild or intense, can look like any or all of these:

- You're eager to grow and expand, but you feel stuck.

- Business is sliding and you don't know why, or how to turn things around.

- Your pricey employees work at cross purposes, or hardly work at all.

- You're not getting paid what you're worth, and may not even be asking.

- You've got a backlog of work so big you've started to hide it.

- You're beginning to have trouble making things happen, and your confidence is taking a hit.

- Resentment and frustration keep flaring up.

- You're beginning to feel burned out, trapped or tapped out.

The typical response to such symptoms is to look for and blame outside factors: "It's gotta be the economy." "We've got all the wrong people working for us." "Our industry is getting hammered these days." "They want to work with younger/older people now, and there's not much you can do about that." "There's something wrong with our marketing."

The last thing most of my clients think about when they're in trouble is the passion at their core. Who has time for something that seems so abstract when you're trying to figure out your next step, or you're in survival mode and stress levels are off the charts?

But if you look again at those telltale signs, you'll notice that in every case, it's as though someone's pulled the plug on momentum, confidence, or even hope. We're looking at an *energy* problem, and recharging the system—that is, YOU—is the only way to find lasting solutions.

DOING THE DIAGNOSTICS: A LOVE/HATE VIEW OF THE PROBLEM

As we go into problem-solving mode in your workplace, let's start with that fundamental question: How much do you love what you do?

Some people just stare blankly at me when I ask, but I've noticed that everyone knows, in detail, what they hate. So I've learned to start there, where the picture is the clearest, and then circle back to the issue of love.

Let me show you how the process of identifying what he hates and loves turned things around for my client Alex, an estate attorney in his late sixties. Alex specializes in handling the planning for small family businesses. It's a niche that's close to his heart, but when he called me, his practice was struggling, and he was feeling desperate.

"I'm not getting any younger, and if I don't start making a lot more money in this business, I'm not going to be able to retire—ever," he told me. "I don't know what's going on. I'm snowed under with work, but we're really struggling. I'm beat. I do everything for these families, and they want me to work for practically minimum wage. I know things have been tight out there, but this is killing me, and I can't see how to turn it around. It's eating me up."

He sagged in his chair as he talked, gripping his pen in his fist.

"Sounds like this is grinding you down," I said.

"Damn straight. It's getting hard to come into the office—that's never happened to me before."

"So why don't you tell me what you really hate about the job," I said. "And be as specific as you can."

He smiled for the first time. "Ha! That's easy. I can't stand the fact that I constantly have to beg people for money. I know their situations inside out, and because of the plans I help them make, they can finally stop worrying about what happens when it's time to pass the operation on to the next generation. They tell me I'm the only one they trust, so they want me to handle every *other* contract they need to sign, even when I let them know it's way outside my specialty. It seems like they never stop asking for another 'special favor.' And dammit, they don't pay me what I'm worth. I'm sick of it."

We wound our way back to what he liked most about his work.

"Some days I can hardly remember," Alex said. "But I always like the meat of what I'm supposed to be doing, the wills and trusts and actual estate planning. I really like the writing and the problem-solving, when I have time to do it right. But I have to do everything so fast now I can't really do my best work, so I can't even take much pride in that. It's knocked me down, that's for sure."

TRY IT YOURSELF: THE LOVE/HATE EXERCISE

Take a minute and write down what you hate about your job, and what you love. There's no one to impress, no gain in hiding. If you're in a basically good place, except for a few annoying bits, be specific about what gets under your skin. And if you're, say, a primary-care physician who hates seeing patients, a divorce attorney who prefers real estate law, or a car salesman who just can't get excited about sales, this is a safe, useful place to admit it. No one will panic, judge you, or be let down. No one but you will see your answers. What's important is to tell yourself the truth.

Maybe what you liked about the job when you started is something you don't do much of anymore. Maybe you got into your vocation because you were pushed into it, or took the path of least resistance, thinking you'd eventually switch gears and choose something that suited you better. Maybe you got very good at something you stopped enjoying years ago. Maybe you just feel as though the thrill is gone. Write it all down: What did you love at the beginning? Are you doing any of that anymore? What did you think/hope you'd be doing? What really happened?

Then remember what it felt or feels like to do the part of the job that excites or satisfies you. What feels like a fit? What, if anything, is easy and fun? If the love is all in the past, what did you once do that you miss doing now?

Don't get hung up or worried if you go blank or your lists seem short, especially if you're wrestling with a problem situation and not easily coming up with positives. This is a starting point, and later in the chapter, I'll show you some tricks for reconnecting with buried passions.

PRESCRIPTION: LESS OF WHAT YOU HATE, MORE OF WHAT YOU LOVE

When you've taken an honest look at what you love and hate about your work situation and how you wound up there, the strategy is simple, though it may not be easy: Aim to maximize the elements you love and minimize the ones you don't. You can do this without drama, a step at a time, though you may well find that even small new choices set major changes in motion.

The simple equation is: Hate it = energy suck = you lose your power to connect. Love it = charging the battery = amping up every connection.

WHY YOU NEED TO DO THIS

The person who knows what he or she likes and thrives doing it is the person you were meant to be, your authentic self. And for many of us, that self doesn't get out a lot. Most people don't even think about it. Their minds and days are focused on the task at hand, which is usually survival. Covering the overhead. Keeping families happy. Paying the bills. Being sure kids and parents have what they need. Those obligations can drive every choice you make. But making decisions because you "have to" or "need to" can easily pull you away from your core. You've got to put a roof over your head, so you have to take a job you're not wild about, or you go into a "money" field that may not suit you. Then you "have to" stay in that job to meet your nut, keep your partner in fancy shoes, pay for the kids' braces, and impress your peers.

It's all too easy to say yes to options that don't suit you because you think there's no other choice.

That road can take you farther and farther from yourself. So far that you stop thinking in terms of prioritizing what you like—or even being sure of what that is.

Authenticity starts with knowing, for yourself, what matters to you. Not what ought to matter, or what your spouse/boss/partner demands that you care about, but what you truly love.

Once you have that clarity again, you have a base for making decisions from a place of integrity and your own personal power. When you're playing your own game, the one you are in this life to master, everything gets easier. You can draw on your strengths, make choices that make you happy, and stop any struggling, lying and pretending.

HOW "YES" BECOMES A LIE, AND HIDING TAKES OVER

Alex saw himself as a man of integrity. Though he was stressed out when we met, he never thought of himself as anything but an honest man. But he'd fallen into a trap that often catches people unaware. As his business began to struggle, Alex's default mode became "yes." He'd grit his teeth, swear under his breath, and agree to take on yet another small job that he knew he couldn't really handle, and didn't want to do. Alex, an estate specialist who can easily craft trusts and creative transition plans for clients, found himself struggling through property contracts and other tasks he wasn't equipped to handle. There was no joy for him in these add-on jobs, just a truckload of resentment about the burden.

The extra money looked good on paper. But the cost was tremendous. The energy drain of the work, and the way it diverted him from his chosen specialty, was pulling his business down. The resentment was costing him too. When you start resenting the people you're in business to serve, no one benefits. More often than he wanted to admit, Alex was turning into an irritable guy who believed he was being taken advantage of. (Just the kind of person everyone wants to do business with, right?) Small wonder he was feeling so stuck.

If you're struggling in some aspect of your business life, I can almost guarantee that one key reason is that, like Alex, you've let yourself believe that you have no choice but to continue to take on or keep doing work you hate. But the more you do that, the more resentment, denial, avoidance, and even despair begin to color everything. You block the energy in your authentic core from flowing into the life you want to lead.

Alex's "yes" problem had another particularly damaging effect. He wound up creating a backlog of work, a long list of tasks that he told no one about and promises he'd made that he couldn't keep anytime soon.

I can't tell you how common this is. In many small firms and businesses, assistants to people like Alex tell me, "I didn't even know we had this deadline. The boss didn't say a word. A client came in looking for something he'd promised them, and we had to scramble like an ambulance had roared in. It didn't have to be an emergency, and we could've helped him get it done on time, but he never said anything about it."

The hidden truth in many operations is that hard-pressed people like Alex are keeping secrets. They lie to themselves about what they like and what they can do, and maintain a facade of "having things under control" by hiding their promises and obligations from their partners, co-workers, employees, and even themselves.

In essence, they start leading a double life: one in which they pretend to be functioning and enjoying what they do, and the real life in which desperation and unhappiness are building, and satisfaction seems light years away.

The danger of losing touch with your authentic self, which is really what we're talking about here, is that until you're living authentically, you *always* have something to hide. When you're authentically connected to your own passions, and energized by them, you can make choices that let you lead one powerful life. When you're not connected to what you love, you may be living ten lives, and staggering under the weight of some very heavy facades. Anytime you're hiding from the truth, you're lying, first to yourself, and eventually to your family, clients, and the world at large. *Hiding is exhausting.*

THE POWER OF THE "NOT TO DO" LIST

Alex's first step out of that trap, I told him, was to make a "Not To Do" list—a list of all the tasks he didn't want to do or wasn't equipped to handle. We started with his current to-do list, which we generated in two stages. First, we created a complete, no-hiding list of everything he needed to do. We started with his "official" to-do list, the tasks he'd written down and shared with the people in his office, then we added a "brain dump" of the tasks he was holding in his head, all those promises, secrets, and nightmare projects that were keeping him up at night.

Simply getting every item written down in one place is a big relief. For many people, it's the first time they can see their situation clearly. "You mean I know how deep the hole is," Alex said.

"I mean you're clear about where you are right now," I said—because you need to know where you stand before you can begin mapping the way to where you really want to be. You can't plan or change course without full disclosure, at least to yourself, about your true status at this moment.

"Once you have a complete list," I told him, "do a simple sort: Anything you like or enjoy, or that challenges you in a positive way, stays on the To Do list. Anything you hate or avoid goes in the Not To Do pile."

Now, instead of blindly assuming he was still stuck with every-thing, he could use the Not To Do list to step back and ask:

- Which of these items is causing me the most headaches and distress?
- What feels like the biggest time and energy suck?
- What can I cancel or give to someone else?
- Who else could handle this?
- What would it take to make that happen?

The clarity that comes from doing this can be scary, which is why so many people avoid it. But it's always transformative, even if you conclude that "this is the way it is, and it's not going to change for now." Admitting that truth will create a shift, because once you share it, everyone will understand what's happening, and why.

TRY IT YOURSELF: THE NOT TO DO LIST

Compile your own complete to-do list, using a brain dump to capture every task, promise, and commitment in one place. Then make your own Not To Do list, and run it through the bullet point list above. Jot down whatever notes you'd like to make about the patterns you see.

I encourage all my clients to do this once a month, often by simply talking to a trusted staff member who can take notes. One stressed entrepreneur told me that business worries had left him with insomnia for more than a year, but he slept like a baby the night after he did his first big info dump. Stress builds behind the secrets you keep, and you'll feel the pressure diminish dramatically when you finally release all you were hiding and get it onto a list.

HONESTY IS A CHANGE ENGINE

Michelle, a lawyer in her thirties, called me because she wanted to grow her firm. She comes from a family of lawyers, and she told me that at a crossroads in her twenties, she'd applied to law school, in case she couldn't find a decent job with her business degree. She'd been sure she'd made a great decision when the economy tanked and she was able to stay afloat by setting up her own practice—she liked being able to control her own destiny. But ten years in, she felt as if she'd hit a wall when she tried, and failed, to expand her business.

"So do you like what you do?" I asked her.

"Truthfully? Well, I like helping people...." she said. I could tell she was sincere, but you couldn't fill a shot glass with the amount of enthusiasm she had in her voice.

We looked closely at what she loved and hated about her work, and when we talked about her Not To Do list, she was stunned to see that many of the tasks she wanted to get rid of had to do with the nuts-and-bolts work of doing research and drafting legal documents. What really energized her was managing the people in the firm and thinking about business strategies. "To be honest," she admitted as we talked, "if someone said I could never practice law again, I'd be just fine with it."

It was no surprise she couldn't grow her business. She didn't want to *do* the work she was trying to bring in. But she probably would've kept bumping along with it forever if she hadn't admitted to herself that her path didn't suit her anymore.

I see this all the time. Discovering and owning your truth brings a powerful clarity. As Michelle told me, "I finally get it. The reason the firm isn't doing better is that I don't want to go on with the law. It's not that I don't have the right people in place or need a better marketing plan or some expensive new strategy. The problem is me: I don't want to do this work."

That acknowledgment gave her a new story about the business—a true story, not a fantasy. Now, instead of trying to patch over imagined problems, she could come to terms with the real ones, and a new set of choices opened up. She's talking about using her knowledge of the law to put together management services for law offices, an idea that's got her energized. The idea is easy for her to sell because it's got her authentic enthusiasm behind it.

Possibilities multiply when the truth is on the table. When my client Charlie let people in his circle know that he intended to stop doing the marketing work that he hated, he was surprised at how fast options appeared. One young staffer came to him and said, "Let me take that on—I love doing it." A colleague suggested that they merge operations, with Charlie handling sales and person-to-person outreach, and the colleague handling marketing strategy. Movement like that is common because honesty triggers action. And the resulting changes can be dramatic. Charlie looked years younger when I talked with him last. "This is how I want to live," he told me. "I love coming to work now, for the first time in years. We're attracting great new clients. And I'm not doing the freakin' marketing plan anymore. I never thought I'd be this happy again."

YOU HAVE TO LOOK <u>INSIDE</u> FIRST

People avoid introspection as long as they can, believing that looking at their *feelings* about their business situation—particularly their anger, fears, and insecurities—will be not just uncomfortable but destructive. They don't want to look or feel vulnerable, and they often have the sense that admitting the truth to themselves, and others, will make them look weak. So they spend their time and money building solutions that work around the real issues. That's like trying to pave a road with the cars still on it. Those buried truths keep popping through.

As I will say again and again in this book, change starts with us, every time. It's an inside job, and inside is often the last place we look. Your connection with yourself is the key to your relationship with everything else, and it's vital to fight the urge to look outside and instead invest the time it takes to get clear with yourself about your real feelings.

THE PASSION CONNECTION

Paring away the activities that don't fit with who you really are clears space for you to tap the energy that naturally fills you when you're engaged with your passions. But what if you no longer know what you love? It's easy to get so focused on your obligations that you put the idea of passion in the closet and forget about it.

That's what happened to Alex, the family-business estate lawyer. When we got through with his Not To Do list, I asked him to think beyond what he liked to do at work and tell me what he was passionate about in his life.

He gave me a puzzled look. "You mean hobbies, like golf or something? I don't do that."

I noticed framed photos of children on his desk. He was in the center of most of them, surrounded by a happy-looking group. I picked up one of the photos and asked, "What's going on here? Must be your grandkids?"

His face lit up. "That's right. I'm with them every chance I can get," he said. "It's funny. They're like the kids I never had. My own kids weren't that interested in hiking and camping, which I love, but *their* kids—they're game for anything. They beg to visit us, and all they want to do is spend time with me. I think their parents are a little jealous of how the kids run straight to me and never look back."

Alex's ten grandchildren clearly adored him. He taught them games, took them on expeditions into the woods, and they'd follow their Poppy anywhere. Alex was relaxed and confident as he talked about a recent visit with his youngest grandchildren, whom he's informally coaching in football. His whole body relaxed.

"There aren't nearly enough hours in the week to spend with them," he said. "It's been a real surprise to me." His face turned serious. "That's what makes this whole financial mess so friggin' bad. If I could straighten it out, I could have more time with them while they're still young."

The Alex who talked about his passion for his grandkids had a huge spirit and overflowed with an energy that wasn't there as he described his business, and when I pointed that out, he said he'd noticed it too. What we needed to do, I told him, was tap some of the freedom he felt with the kids and find a way for him to be that charismatic Pied Piper with his clients.

When he was Poppy, he was fully in touch with the pleasure and aliveness of being active in the outdoors, playing and teaching. He could take off his suit, kick back, and, without the B.S. of being a lawyer, just have a good time being in his own skin, doing what he liked. When he relaxed into that, a whole tribe of kids wanted whatever he had to offer.

"Great," Alex said. "So my grandkids love me. But they're kids. I work with adults, and I don't see how this is relevant."

"You're forgetting something important," I told him. "Kids are more in tune with energy and authenticity than adults are because they don't have shields and filters up. They know what they like and who they trust, and they won't follow just anyone. They haven't built up the crap adults have. You can't fool kids—if you're just going through the motions, they know it."

"I can't argue with that, but I still don't see where you're going with this," Alex grumbled. "I don't see myself going, 'Hey clients, let's go play in the woods.'"

No need to, I told him. The point of knowing and reconnecting with what gives you energy is to feel it again, and then to bring the *essence* of it, a way of being that you've left outside the job, into your work environment.

MAKING THE PASSION CONNECTION

I encouraged Alex to look at the person he let himself be when he was with his grandkids—confident, brimming with energy. This was a person his clients rarely, if ever, saw. With them, particularly when it was time to talk about his fees, he clenched up and often became defensive or apologetic.

That was significant, because one of his biggest problems was that he couldn't ask clients for what he needed—and what he was worth. He's in a specialized niche, and he's exceptionally creative, yet he could only bring himself to charge $10,000 to $12,000 for a job that took $50,000 to $60,000 worth of work. "Listen, Alex," I told him. "Those families will spend sixty grand on one piece of equipment, or even on another car. You're taking care of their whole family, and looking out for the long-term security of their children and grandchildren. You need to own that expertise, just the way you do when you're being Poppy in the woods, leading your tribe and commanding their respect, by being who you naturally are."

Being relaxed, natural, and connected to your authentic self isn't about not being serious, and I wasn't suggesting that Alex frolic in the office. "Authentic" means being in the moment with his clients, free of all the self-criticism that kept him apologizing when he needed to lead.

I suggested that he practice bringing his "Poppy" energy into the office by consciously feeling it in his body, where so much of our authenticity resides. Before meeting with clients, I asked him to picture being in the woods with his grandkids, and to let that energy fill him up. *That* guy was the one who needed to walk into client meetings.

It took some work, but once Alex got the hang of it, he stopped leaving his best self behind when it was time to ask for what he wanted, and a new kind of ease came into his relationships with clients. He stopped undercutting himself, and a genuine joy came into his work. The amazing thing was, all that change started when he connected to himself.

DRILLING DOWN: WHAT MAKES YOU PASSIONATE ABOUT YOUR PASSIONS?

As we saw with Alex, the things you love the most in life may seem to have nothing to do with business. You may say, "I really love football. How in the heck is that related to my job?"

But if you know how to look, you'll find the elements that could re-energize even the most stalled-seeming scenarios. The trick is to look for what you love about the activity or part of life you're passionate about, and the way it makes you feel.

Start by thinking about your own interests, whatever moves the needle for you. My client Ted, a web designer who was feeling restless and stuck at work, is a rabid USC football fan, so that was a natural place to start when we began looking for his sources of passion and enthusiasm. When I asked what specifically lit him up about watching his team, he told me: "I love the strategy in the game. And I really love being in the stadium—the crowd, the bands, everything. There's something about the mix of brute strength and drive, everybody moving in the same direction, the action in the stands cheering it all on. It takes me back to how free I felt in college. And there's so much freedom on that field, so many variables. I could watch it forever and never get tired of it, especially out there with the crazy fans."

"Okay," I said. "That's awesome. How much of that feeling do you have going on at your office right now?"

"You have got to be kidding me," Ted said.

"No, seriously. How much of that feeling is in your workplace?"

"None. Not one bit," he said.

"So how can we bring it in?"

Once you know what energizes, inspires and engages you, the next step is to find ways to carry that essence into your job. Start by asking: Knowing what I know right now about the experience I love the most, what do I need to do to create the same feeling at work?

Ted thought a moment about that question. "Something about the crowd experience really stays with me," he said.

"You like the energy of being around people?"

"Oh yeah, and the funny thing is that I work by myself most of the time. I like being part of something big, so how the hell did I end up in a two-person office, with a guy who doesn't like to talk?"

In a case like that, I suggest immediate small steps: getting out of the office and interacting with people a couple of times a week. Or for a person who works alone, hiring an assistant to come into the office to begin to crack the feeling of isolation. It could be that joining a larger operation would provide some of the feeling that's missing.

Ted hadn't been considering any of this, but once he tuned into the energized feeling of a Trojan game, he knew what he was aiming for. "What I've realized is that I like a team culture," he told me. "I'd been turning down people who wanted me to work with them because I had it in my head that I wanted to build something of my own. But you know what? It ain't me."

When I work with people to ask these questions and help them reconnect to their inner spark, I'm not creating a new path for them. I'm helping them uncover the path that's true to them, a path they *already know*. It's always wired directly to who they really are and what they love. Not *should* love, or tolerate because there's no other choice, but genuinely care about.

That's where the power is.

BRINGING AUTHENTICITY INTO EVERYDAY DECISION-MAKING: MAKING YES MEAN YES

As you get clear about what you love and hate and what you want more and less of in your workplace, it gets harder to go along blindly saying "yes" to requests, obligations and opportunities that don't fit with your authentic desires. That's as it should be. One of the most life-changing steps you can take is to learn to say yes only when you mean it, and to hold firm when you say no. It's no simple thing. You could fill a book with the reasons people say yes, many of them having nothing at all to do with what they really want.

As we saw with Alex above, "yes" can become a security blanket that supposedly guarantees more money. Or it can be a way of trying to look like a Superman who can do it all, even when what's on offer is kryptonite. We say yes to please and placate and buy affection, to "help someone out," to prove our indispensability. We do it for love and out of habit.... As I said, you could fill a book with reasons, many of which have nothing to do with "I want to because of who I am."

But the stronger your connection to yourself, the more urgent it begins to feel to let people see who you are, and deal with the authentic you. Suddenly, you can see what the "automatic yes" has cost you, and with that can come remorse and regret. Go gently in the beginning as you size up the legacy of all the yeses you didn't mean. Start by easing in. What would you have done differently?

Why did you want to say no? Why didn't or couldn't you?

One of my clients, Ben, was in a business that was doing very well—just not well enough to support his lifestyle. As we talked, he traced the struggles he was having to a single "yes."

"Fifteen years ago we were really doing well," he said. "Then my wife fell in love with our current house. It doubled our mortgage payment, and I didn't want to do it. But the house was so amazing, and it made her so happy, that I went along with it. She still loves the place, but we are strapped to it, and we can't afford to do a lot of things we'd like to. If we had stayed in our old house, I'd have kept half a mil in the bank and by now, it would probably have been a million and a half. We could travel, I could pay for my kid's wedding, and we wouldn't be having this struggle every day to just keep the lights on."

Ben is sure that if he tells his wife the strain of carrying this burden is too much for him, she'll freak out, and their whole life will fall apart. So I didn't ask him to go home and confess his fears and struggles to her just to make himself feel better. As we'll see in later chapters, it's possible to develop effective strategies for readjusting the balance and repairing the broken connections in situations like this, but the first step is what Ben was doing: being authentic with yourself.

COULD YOU START BEING HONEST WITH YOURSELF RIGHT NOW?

I suggested that before bringing up the high-stakes house decision with his wife, Ben could first work on raising the level of authenticity in the rest of his life. "If you had to start being completely authentic right now, could you do it?" I asked. "If not, why not? And if you could, if you started today, what could the positive result be?"

For some people, considering that prospect is like getting out of jail, and like Ben, they're eager to get going. I advise them—and you, if you're game—to think about the choices in your life that you have sole control over. In this category are probably things like whether you snack at night or stay up late surfing the Internet. Whether you drive or take public transportation to work. Perhaps what time you leave work and how you deploy your schedule. In the arena you control, ask again: Could you give your "yes" power again by only using it when you mean it, and only when it serves your authentic self?

The first thing that occurred to Ben was that he was feeling stressed and burned out, and wanted to go home at a reasonable hour and spend time with his family instead of staying at the office until eight or nine p.m. Could he stop saying "yes" to a schedule that had never worked for him? He decided to tell his secretary that he was going to go home every day at five, and that no one was to schedule him beyond four-thirty. He'd be able to see his kids, have dinner with the family, and if he needed to work a while in the evening, at least he'd feel refreshed.

When the world didn't fall apart at that change, he began to make others. *Any* small change driven by an authentic "yes" can lead to something that works better, and the simple act of being available to his wife and family opened the way for major shifts when he was ready.

You don't have to go back and reprocess every "yes" you regret to move forward in a way that's connected to your self. Take it slowly. If you suddenly start saying "no" after thirty years of being an automatic-yes man, you'll probably feel like you're standing in the middle of Times Square naked. Vulnerability is part of being authentic, but you can pace yourself as you work toward it—and you should.

I want to make it very clear that saying "yes" only when you mean it is not about being self-absorbed or narcissistic. It's about actively choosing your authentic self. As Shore Slocum, the motivational speaker, puts it so well: The more you say YES to the things you really want to say NO to, the farther you get away from your authentic self. The more you say YES to the things you really want to say YES to and NO to the things you really want to say NO to, the closer you get your authentic self. Choose wisely to become the person you most want to be.

This is hard work. You need it to be safe.
And you may need a hand.

Keep this in mind: A good number of the people you know—your peers, your friends—look great on the outside, but what's going on inside is a different story. The pressure to "never let them see you sweat" is intense, as is the pressure we feel as adults to be able to handle things on our own. Even when we're on the edge, many of us don't say a word to our families and friends, and no one has a clue about the battles we're fighting.

One consequence of that is that we make things many times more difficult for ourselves because we don't admit the reality of our struggles, even to ourselves. Being honest with yourself puts you in a vulnerable place that a lot of us would do almost anything to avoid. Because sometimes it looks like the whole house of cards will fall down if you get real. What if you've built a whole life, a whole career, around something you never truly wanted, or grew out of? What if you need a do-over? What if your truth is that you can't go on living the lie that things are just fine?

Even considering that possibility sets off alarms.

So I always tell my clients to ask themselves: How can I make it safe for myself to look at the truth of my life? I like to go into the mountains and hike as I think, because nature inspires and recharges me. Looking out at the vista of a forest gives me the confidence that some of the force that built all that is inside me, and if I slow down enough, I can tap it.

Many people reinforce their sense of support and safety at church or in temple, or by talking with a friend or coach. Through this process, you need at least one ear you can trust.

If you're the person at the top of your business, you may feel pretty isolated. I don't care how brilliant you are, you need to surround yourself with people who will listen to you, help you, and tell you the truth. On the journey of self-reflection that our work with connection requires, you need to be able to admit your concerns, your fears, and most of all your truth. But you can't do that with someone who's dependent on the outcome of your decisions. A CEO can't tell his board he's freaking out. A solo practitioner doesn't have a natural place to go.

So your top priority is to find someone with whom you can be honest, someone who's not dependent on the outcome of your decisions or will project their own fears or worries onto you. You want a neutral, objective party so you don't have to manage his or her fear and dysfunction as well as your own. Don't confide in someone whose worry you'll have to manage as you make new decisions about moving forward.

I know many of you are used to holding your cards close to the vest, but you can make things much easier on yourself if you find a sounding board. Most people need help with this kind of self-exploration. It's new. It can be painful. It ain't easy. So seek out a coach or mastermind group if you need one, or turn to the person in your life who always has your back. You don't have to go it alone.

TOOLS FOR THE ROAD: STRENGTHENING CONNECTION TO THE SELF

The work we've done so far will definitely connect you to your authentic self. To keep that connection strong, I recommend working with the tools below. They'll show and remind you of the self who's your best guide through life.

1. Collect stories that answer the question: When have you felt most alive?

Think about a time in your life when it felt as though all the best parts of yourself were right there, visible and working. It might've been during a vacation you took as a child, or in a love relationship, or when you were traveling.

When I ask clients to do this, I often hear stories like these:

"I was eight years old, fishing in a river with my grandfather and just goofing around, when I hooked a huge fish. It had never happened before. I was nervous and excited and also very calm as I listened to my grandpa talk me through reeling it in. I remember how I didn't know if I could keep my grip on the pole, but I just stayed with it, and I kept watching that fish jumping and flashing in the sun. When I got it up close and my grandpa helped me with that final few feet I was barely in my skin, I was so excited and proud."

"I was skiing and I got lost in the woods. It was getting dark, but the moon was coming up and I could tell it would be bright enough to see. It was frigid, and I couldn't afford to be out there too long, so I picked a route down and got moving. I'll never forget the way the snow looked in the moonlight or how loud my heart sounded in my ears. I was scared, but somehow I knew I'd be okay. Finally I saw a trail sign and knew where I was, and when I got to the bottom, I was elated, and so glad that this crazy thing happened to me."

There's a kind of aliveness that comes through in these memories, and connecting with it can bring you back to the feeling of the person you are underneath all the roles you play, and remind you of what feeds that. Take some time to gather some of your own "peak experience" stories, moments large and small. Your body and spirit will remember them as your mind plays them back to you. You don't have to analyze them, just feel them. They'll throw you back into a sense of being fully present, awake to what's inside and around you. That kind of aliveness is what a strong connection to your authentic self feels like.

What can you do to nurture it? Spend time alone? Go into nature? Take more physical risks? Connect with an encouraging partner or mentor? What feeds all the best parts of you? How can you do it more?

2. Establish a daily practice of tuning in to yourself.

It takes effort to stay connected with yourself in the rush, stress, and competing priorities of everyday life. That's why I recommend that you have a daily practice of renewing the connection. Here's what that daily practice can look like:

First, start your day with gratitude.

A lot of people wake to an alarm and start running. How do you set what's going to happen in your day? You may have a list swarming through your head from the moment you wake: Go to work, get the car fixed, take the kids to practice, clean the house. But on a deeper level, what are you here to do today? What do you need?

I suggest that the first thing you do in the morning is tell yourself what you're grateful for. That won't take you away from the realities you have to deal with, but it will help you connect to your deeper purpose for doing what you'll be doing during the day.

It can be as quick as this thought: "I know I'm going to be jammed all week. Why the hell am I killing myself? Because I have this woman I love, who's sleeping beside me, these kids I cherish, and this house I've poured myself into fixing up."

Next, remember to "check out" a couple of times a day.

By that I mean shut everything off—the phones, the computer, the conversations with the people in the office. For even five minutes, disconnect from the pressure and the craziness around you and ask yourself, "What do I need right now? How can I feed myself?" What pops to mind may be as simple as "I just need to get outside for a minute." If you do highly detailed work, you may need to zone out by watching a funny video, but I don't recommend surfing the Internet. It's more effective to pull yourself back into your body and see what the body wants. Often, just breathing a little, and taking a quick walk around the block, can bring back your sense of who you are outside your assigned title and roles. You might want to call your girlfriend to hear her voice, or stare at the clouds. The more you ask, "What do I need?" the easier it is to know.

Note that "What do I need right now?" is a very different question from "What do I have to do next?"

What do you need? Don't overthink it. This is not deep contemplation. Just ask, let an answer come, and see what happens. Don't judge your responses, and don't be surprised if nothing comes to you at first. Listening to yourself is a muscle you have to work a little to develop. After twenty years of parenting or partnering or being a team player, you may be out of practice at paying attention to what's going on inside you. But being aware of your genuine needs and wants in the moment is an act of kindness to yourself, an act of love.

Sometimes, you won't know at first what will make you happy. One of my default settings is that food is a good solution to any problem, and at the end of a stressful day, I may find myself in front of the refrigerator with a pint of ice cream in my hand. Just stopping then to say, "What do I need right now?" connects me with what I'm feeling—and often, it isn't hunger. It might be "I need a hug" or "I need to smash something" or "I need to blast some music."

Finding out gets easier the more you tune in.

3. Keep asking the question: "What do I love?"

Identifying and connecting with your passions isn't a one-time event. It's a process that acknowledges that your interests and concerns today may be far different than they were ten or twenty years ago, or even last week. Checking in with yourself every day is vital in part because it helps you stay current with yourself. This work is not about reaching specific conclusions and cementing them into your life, but about staying open to the possibilities all around you, and letting your interests or curiosities or fascinations draw you to them. When you keep yourself open to situations, your perception changes. The way people approach you changes. You step into a flow of opportunities that may have been invisible to you in the past because you were so consumed with the struggle to like and do things that drain you. There's a kind of magic in pulling away from all that, but it can be disconcerting. Suddenly, you're "living in the in-between," as I sometimes call it, a place in which you don't know how your grand experiment with using your authentic self as a compass will turn out.

Take a chance. My experience, and that of my clients, has shown me that staying open, and aligned with your passions and purpose, will take you exactly where you need to go.

CHAPTER 2

The Avoidance Trap

We talked in the last chapter about how connection gives you the power to move your plans and dreams forward. You saw just how much energy becomes available when you allow yourself to focus on what you love to do and bring your authentic enthusiasm, the essence of your best self, into your work life.

But we don't operate in a vacuum. The changes and choices we make often involve other people. And other people complicate everything. Those "complications" can be both wonderful and problematic, and they can profoundly affect the way you connect to your authentic self.

Humans are social creatures. We want to be liked so clients will hire us, people will buy what we're selling, and our partners will keep giving us love. We often have the idea that "like me" is a fire we need to keep stoking. So we may pile on gifts and attention—and compromises—because we think that's the way to be what our partners want us to be. We often put them first, minimizing what *we* need, so they'll stay interested and supportive. With our loved ones, we compromise so they'll be happy and we'll be the reason for their smiles. When kids enter the picture, we want to give them the best life we can, and be the kind of parent we always wanted to have. That, too, can mean putting our desires behind theirs.

None of this is bad. But often, all this giving is interwoven with an unconscious belief: *They're not going to love/like/hire/promote me if I don't let them have what they want.* That thought goes hand in hand with this troublemaker: *They'd reject me if they found out that I'm an independent person who has needs and desires that don't involve them.* And this one: *They'll freak out if I let on that I need their support.*

It's all too easy to wind up sacrificing your authenticity to such fears. But the truth is, personal relationships are powered by your connection to your authentic self, which is quirky, imperfect, and ever-evolving. You can't and won't have the relationships you want if you give up the biggest, wildest, most creative parts of yourself, or chain yourself to a job or way of being that's flattening you with stress. Neglect your own happiness, passions, interests, and aliveness—even if you think you're doing it for the sake of love—and your life will be hollow. Not to mention lonely.

Because the stakes are so high and clear, and the compromises are so apparent in love relationships, the examples in this chapter focus there. But you'll see the same dynamics in relationships with your boss, employees, clients, and friends. If you're one of the many people who've misplaced their clear perspective on what they want and need, and what it's possible to have in a relationship, the tools you'll find in this chapter will show you, step by step, how to get it back.

The biggest gift you can give other people is your authenticity. In this chapter, I'll show you how to get and stay connected to it in the field (and sometimes it's a minefield) of personal relationships.

EIGHT SYMPTOMS THAT YOUR AUTHENTIC SELF HAS GONE MISSING IN YOUR RELATIONSHIPS

Authenticity is a state of being in which your actions reflect your feelings, beliefs and desires. You are who you are, and the person you are on the outside looks like the one on the inside. The false fronts have fallen, and the engine driving your life is a desire to bring all the best parts of yourself into play. People who love *this* person are getting the real thing.

We're all works in progress, and I'm not saying for a minute that you have to have this authenticity thing perfectly mastered before you can have strong relationships. You do, though, have to be willing to keep working toward it—and know when it's slipping away.

The number one sign that you've lost or are losing your connection to yourself when dealing with other people is avoidance. Rather than admitting what's true for you when a conflict, disagreement, or thorny issue arises, you find a way to delay addressing it. You may pretend that the conflict doesn't exist, even when it's eating you up inside. Because maybe if you put off facing it, it'll just go away.

It's significant that we can see avoidance at work in so many of the symptoms below, which signal that you're not acting on your own truth—and may even be losing track of what that is:

- Your partner/family's behavior is causing you a great deal of stress, but you don't mention it because you don't want to make waves.

- You've started to isolate yourself at home and retreat into your bedroom, your garage, or your computer.

- You're having trouble making decisions about what you need to do next in your situation. You feel stuck.

- You rarely, if ever, talk about your own needs. (Needs? What needs?) And no one seems to ask.

- Your partner/family/colleagues know exactly how to push your buttons and get what they want from you—and you're getting weary of it.

- The only way you can get people to take you seriously is to yell.

- You're afraid of what will happen if you say how you really feel about what's going on, so you don't say a word.

– You don't fight with your partner/family anymore. You pay the bills and stay out of the fray.

Avoidance pushes your truth to the side, and every time you choose it, you subtly erode your connection to yourself and close down your intuition and emotions. A subtle dishonesty sets in. You're not being a bad person, but you're no longer making decisions the way you want to. And if avoidance becomes a habit, as it often does, it can sabotage your very sense of who you are.

THE AVOIDANCE CHAIN

I'll show you how this works by telling the story of Jesse, a composite character based on several of my clients. Jesse, a Realtor, was struggling to stabilize his business after he and a partner had a falling out. After months of work, he had expanded into office leasing, and was feeling optimistic about his prospects. But when I asked him what was going on at home, he was oddly downbeat.

"Grace, my wife, is really making things tough for me," he said. "She ought to know how bad things have been and how careful we need to be with money while I make this transition. I couldn't believe it when she brought home a $500 purse last week and was so proud of herself because she got it 'on sale.' It was just unbelievable."

"So what did you tell her?" I asked.

"Well this is the thing," he said after a pause. "I was ready to kill her. But she gave me a big hug and said she was really proud of the way I'd turned things around in the business, and I just didn't have the energy for a big scene."

"So you didn't say anything?"

He shook his head. "And now there's another $500 on our credit card bill that we just can't afford."

For Jesse, the honest, authentic response would've been to say, "Honey, business has turned around in a big way and I'm proud of that. But we've got a ways to go, and I don't want to take on the expense of that purse right now." Or simply to say, "Grace, that's a beautiful purse, but we can't afford it."

The big problem with skirting the issue and letting his frustration, stress, and debt build, is that avoidance snowballs. When Jesse tells himself, "I don't want to fight about this. I'm just going to pay the frickin' bill because I can't deal with her upset," a few things happen:

- He hides his true feelings from his wife, and, in the name of making her happy, he throws distance between them. Every time he says "yes" when he adamantly means "no," he closes himself off from her.

- He tells himself, "That worked! There was no fight. This is a good strategy for keeping the peace." Therefore he sets himself up for a self-reinforcing avoidance loop as his debt and resentment grow.

- He hides from himself. Unconsciously, he may feel ashamed that he can't buy Grace anything she wants, which triggers thoughts like, "I should make more money. I'm not successful. I'm a loser." There can be deep pain tied up with that train of thought, and like Jesse, many people will use avoidance to numb themselves. Unfortunately, when the "anesthesia" wears off, the pain is still there. And the problem that triggered it is much larger.

I want to emphasize that there's no one right response to a situation like this. Your truth may be different from Jesse's when it comes to a spouse's spending. Your deepest feeling might be: "God, this purse makes the woman I love so happy that even though we can't afford it, I want her to have it. I think I can make a few calls and drum up some extra business."

Money is a hot-button issue, and men are quick to blame women for overspending. It's easy to look at the bills, do the math and say, "What the heck is she thinking? How could this happen?" And that may or may not be an authentic response. Authenticity is not about being controlling, and it doesn't mean grabbing your partner by the arm and saying, "Look, this can't happen again!"

Being authentic means letting people know what you're really comfortable with, and what you're not.

To do that, you first need to have a clear understanding of your true feelings, and where the boundary between comfortable/not comfortable is for you.

WHAT DO YOU WANT MORE OF? AND LESS OF?

In the business scenarios we saw in chapter 1, it was fairly simple to come up with a list of what you hate doing, and what you love, in your work life. But the emotions that come with personal relationships can cloud your vision and add a layer of uncertainty.

The most effective tool I've found to bring clarity to my clients' sense of what they want more of and less of in their personal lives is a list of questions that filter any difficult situation through the Four Rs: Regret, Resentment, Respect, and Requests.

Clarity is the first casualty when you don't know how to connect your authentic self at home and in intimate relationships. The Four Rs will help you recover it. As you'll see, these categories will help you get to the essence of what's working and not working in your dealings with loved ones. A further layer of questions will help you see what you want your next steps to be. From there, you can decide what you want to do, and not do. (A friend who went through addiction counseling described the Four Rs process to me years ago, and I don't know where it originated, but I've used it with excellent results, and much gratitude toward its creator.)

USING THE FOUR RS

After the purse incident, Jesse realized how costly his avoidance had become. So we walked through the Four Rs process to begin mapping out a strategy for becoming more authentic in his conversations with Grace, especially the ones around money.

Here's how he used the questions.

Question 1: What decisions have you made in this situation that you truly regret?

"I'd have to say that my biggest regret is that I haven't let Grace and me be a team on the money front," Jesse said. "I told myself that I could handle everything and I've been pretending that I'm some kind of wizard who can make everything all better. I thought it would make things worse to talk about what's going on, so we've gone on as if it's business as usual. The purse thing was an eye-opener. I can see that she really doesn't get our situation. And I let that happen. We used to be so close, but we're almost on different planets now. I truly regret that. I regret giving myself ulcers too. I guess you could say I regret being an idiot."

Your regrets will give you a lot of insight into what you'd most like to change. Remember that this exercise isn't about sliding into a swamp of remorse or sweeping every regret from your whole life into one sad pile. Just look at the one situation in your relationship that you've chosen to work on right now.

Think about not only what you regret, but also *why* you regret it. That will help you pinpoint the costs of the decisions you've made. The big idea, I told Jesse, isn't to beat yourself up or call yourself names. It's to get clarity.

Question 2A: What do you resent about the way other people are behaving in this situation?

Resentments corrode connection. They pile up, often unspoken, and energy that could go into problem solving and closeness gets drained away in bitterness and anger.

Jesse had quite a list of smoldering resentments against Grace: "I hate to admit it, but it really ticks me off to think about how Grace kept on talking about expensive trips she wanted us to take and never let the credit card stay in her wallet for long, even when my business was blowing up. I feel like I'm supposed to be the magic cash machine! How could she not see how stressed I've been? I want her to be happy, but I really resent the way she kept on chattering about her yoga classes or some new outfit she wanted and never even seemed to notice I couldn't sleep and was tied in knots for so long. I want to be able to trust her to take some of the responsibility for our finances, but I don't feel like I can. A $500 purse—come *on*."

Jesse knew that he hadn't spoken frankly about the finances with his wife, but he was fuming about how she hadn't read his mind. Our reasoning often goes that if someone loves us, they must *know* how we're feeling, or when they've crossed the line into hurtful behavior, and we shouldn't have to say anything.

But one of the big drawbacks of disconnecting from your authentic self is that people don't know when you're "acting." They believe what you say and do, especially if it gives them something they want. Your genuine reaction, anger and resentment, often boils in the background, silently adding even more tension and distance to the relationship. If you want to restore connection, it's essential to own up to those feelings.

As you write about your resentments, keep in mind that this exercise isn't a bitch fest, and it's not about being the guy who complains about everything. It's about looking honestly at what is going on, and pulling out all the bad feelings you've stuffed in the closet so you can see them clearly.

Question 2B: What was my part in the situation? How did my behavior play a part in what others did, or even encourage them to behave in the ways I resent?

It can be almost reflexive for some people to take the victim role in a situation like Jesse's. If you're strapped for cash and your wife buys a designer dress, or your husband decides it's time for a new guitar, or your kids throw tantrums because they can't get the newest iPhone, it's not unusual to be frustrated and hurt by how they "want what they want, no matter what."

But people who are really in love with their partners may have made all kinds of deals with themselves that the partner knows nothing about, and have lists of things they think they have to do to make everyone happy. Often the deal is never discussed, but it sets up the rules for the relationship. As Jesse and I talked, it came out that his "deal" with Grace was "I'll be the provider and see that you never have to worry about money. In fact, we won't even talk about it." Her part of the bargain, as he saw it, was to stay with him and stand by him.

"So you haven't told her anything about how much pressure you're under?" I asked. "Do you even know if she really expects you to be the sole provider?"

"Well, she talks sometimes about becoming a yoga instructor, but she hasn't signed up for any program. She was working as a decorator when I met her, but she quit when we got married. I wanted her to. And I've told her as little as possible about the business crap. I figured she'd freak out if I said anything, so I keep it light," Jesse said.

"So let's get back to the question: What part of the situation do you need to own?"

"The whole stoic thing, really. It's not her fault if she's not a mind reader. I haven't come out and told her how bad things have been, and I haven't said no to anything she wants for a long, long time, so why would she want to acknowledge there was a problem? That might've worked once, when times were flusher, but not now. The worst thing is, I feel like there's a lot of unspoken stuff between us because there's so much I keep from her. That's definitely me, not her."

A lot of us can create a mess all by ourselves, and it's easy to resent other people for playing by rules that *you* put in place. But the question, "What's my part in this?" can be a game-changer, because it helps you see how much you've been actively helping create the situation, and how you might change that.

Question 3: What do I respect about the way I've been behaving?

Getting honest as you reconnect to your authentic self doesn't mean beating yourself up. As you look at what is, you won't just see regrets. You'll also see yourself acting in ways that you're proud of, ways that feel solidly connected to your values. Acknowledging those choices brings balance to your assessment of the situation.

"One thing I can say is that I totally respect myself for coming up with a new way forward in my business when things fell apart with my partner," Jesse said. "I didn't panic, I didn't run away—I made myself go out and talk to people, even before the shock had worn off, and I realized that I could do some good business in office leasing. I was scared as hell, but I did it anyway. I'm not a quitter. I kept finding a way to pay the bills, kept taking care of my family. I respect myself for putting one foot in front of the other and not giving up."

The "respect" list helps you see the strengths and values you can put into play to change your situation, and Jesse's list was golden. The same courage he used in his business ("didn't panic" "scared ... but did it anyway," "not a quitter") is available to him as he deals with Grace, and moves toward his goal of getting himself and his wife on the same page again regarding their finances. The resourcefulness he used to come up with a new business model is also something he can tap.

Jesse is very clear about how important it is to take care of his family. The question for him will be: How can he do it in a way that will reduce his regrets and resentments? How can he use his strengths, the traits he respects, as he does that?

Question 4: Knowing what I know now about my regrets, resentments, and what I respect in myself, what do I want to request from myself and the other people in this situation?

Now that you've looked at your situation through the lens of the first three Rs, you can zero in on what you really want in your situation, and what you're willing to ask of yourself and other people to get it.

Look at your list of regrets. What will you ask yourself to do differently to keep from creating more of them?

For Jesse, a couple of big things jumped out: "I'm going to ask myself to stop pretending I can do it all. I want to let Grace know what's really going on, and how much I want her support. I'm going to need some help figuring out what to say, and I'm going to get it, maybe from you," he said. "I'm going to ask myself to re-member that I don't have to cave when the going gets rough, or if she cries or yells or asks what the hell is going on. If she gets upset, that's her right. But it doesn't have to mean I'm going to keep up the lies. I'm going to ask myself to man up and share the truth with the woman I love. I don't want to scare her, but I want to let her know I need her on my team."

Next, look at your list of resentments. What will you ask the other people in the situation to do differently to help you keep from creating more of them?

"This is not going to be easy," Jesse said, "but I am going to ask her to help me make a plan for our spending, which will mean we both figure out what's really important, and what we can save for, or even decide we don't need. Things like that purse. I don't even know the last time we talked about a budget. When we were first married, she got such a kick out of stretching my paychecks. It's been a long time, but maybe she'll remember that. The other thing is, I'm going to ask her to check in with me once in a while and ask me how things are really going. I get all bottled up. I'll just let her know it's okay to ask, and I want her to. Then I won't have to resent it when she doesn't know. It might get us talking again. I miss that."

The plan that emerged for Jesse was far different from the one he might've pushed toward if he followed his original impulse to blame Grace for all of his anger and frustration. When Jesse worked up the courage to tell her about his money concerns, she was shocked at first, but quickly switched into problem-solving mode. He hadn't mentioned the purse, but one of the first things she offered was, "Well, I've been doing a lot of shopping lately, and I can take a few things back."

"This has all been such a relief," Jesse told me. "She wants to sit down and map out a family budget, and she's totally excited about doing something with her yoga. I thought this could tear us apart, but we're talking in a way we haven't in ages. I can't believe I was so afraid of being real with her."

TRY IT YOURSELF: APPLYING THE FOUR RS

Look at an unresolved situation in your personal life, one in which you're avoiding taking action because you don't want to deal with messy feelings—yours or other people's. Run the scenario through the Four Rs, answering the questions above and following the additional instructions. Pick one or two small shifts you can make with no drama or big announcements and experiment with cutting the number of new regrets and resentments you create in the next week. What requests can you make of yourself to help make that happen?

THE NOT TO DO LIST

Chances are, if you've run a problem through the 4 Rs, your perspective has changed. Now, instead of letting blind frustration and resentment drive you, you have a fuller picture of what's really going on, and the part you've played in it. You're connected with your truth, and you're much clearer about what you want. Sit with that a while. You don't have to rush in and change anything right now. In fact, I'd advise you not to before you have a few more tools for connecting to and communicating from your authentic self.

For now, step back and watch yourself and the other people in the situation. And begin to create a Not To Do list based on what you see in the 4 Rs.

The Not To Do list, similar to the one you saw in the last chapter, is a list of things you're no longer willing to do, or know you should not be doing anymore, in a particular relationship or small set of relationships. Behavior you regret belongs on the Not To Do list, as do choices that lead to resentments. Some items you came up with as requests will be a clear fit on the list as well.

Then do a little more self-reflection. If you're a person who's been a human shock absorber for all the people in your life, what do you need to stop doing to lighten that too-heavy load? What activities that you used to love are now tiresome? What deals have you made in your relationship that don't make sense anymore?

What choices and activities are keeping you from meeting your own needs?

Using the Not To Do List makes room for *you* in your life and relationships, and it can include items such as:

- I resent it when people assume I'm going to pick up the tab—so I'm going to stop it and say, "Let's split this."

- I'm going to stop treating my wife like she'll break if I tell her the truth about my business.

- I'm going to quit golfing so my girlfriend and I can travel more—I'm tired of golf.

- We're going to stop spending all weekend with my extended family so I can do things I want to do.

- I want to stay off the Internet in the evening and make more time for being with my kids.

It's possible to fill your life with activities you're doing purely out of habit instead of joy or interest. Making this Not To Do List will help you bring your life up to date. What can you eliminate to make room for what you enjoy? What ancient obligation is no longer serving its original purpose? There will always be garbage to take out, pets to feed, cars to get serviced. I'm not suggesting that we chuck out our responsibilities. But I *am* suggesting that we examine them, and satisfy ourselves that we should still be taking them on. Walk your dog? Sure. Have a weekly breakfast with those frat brothers whose company you stopped enjoying years ago? Maybe not.

THE UNCONSCIOUS YES

We talked in the last chapter about the importance of making yes mean yes. The same principles and practices apply in personal life as in business, and I encourage you to carry them into your home life. It's impossible to be authentic if you divorce your "yes" and "no" from your genuine desires. But in the realm of personal relationships particularly, there's a fuzzy middle ground, a no man's land where nothing is fully discussed or considered, and everything is implied. You enter it every time you use what I call the Unconscious Yes.

The Unconscious Yes takes the form of a distracted nod or a "Sure, whatever you say." You don't really focus on what's being suggested, you simply go along without questioning, resisting, or engaging. You think you're in a holding pattern, but the other person hears a "Yes, let's do it." And that way leads to trouble.

REENGAGING TO END THE UNCONSCIOUS YES

Ed, a contractor, had been using an Unconscious Yes for months with his wife Sarah, whose dream was to buy a place in Oregon and open a bed and breakfast. Ed had nodded as Sarah talked about her plans for them to convert a house and operate the B&B, and he'd played along as she asked him to taste breakfast recipes and look at the quilts and furniture she was considering on eBay.

But recently, he'd started worrying that he—and they—were getting in over their heads. "The thing is, she has a million ideas, and maybe one in a thousand turns into something. I don't think that's a fault—it's something I love about her, the enthusiasm she has for everything, and her imagination. She's creative in a way I'll never be. But there was the time she wanted chickens, so we built a coop out back, and then she got tired of the work so I took it apart. Then she decided she was going to get into smoking meats as a side business, and she couldn't stop talking about it—until she read something about that kind of curing as being bad for health and she lost interest. I thought the B&B was one of those flash-in-the-pan things.

"When she started talking about going up to Oregon to look at properties, though, I realized she's serious. Holy shit. I have no interest in going to Oregon to change sheets and make muffins. Are you kidding me? I'm a builder, not a maid service. But what am I supposed to say, 'Hon, I wasn't paying attention all that time, and now I am and I don't want to do it?' She'll kill me."

The Unconscious Yes is a common form of avoidance, and Ed had been avoiding taking Sarah's B&B plan seriously even as he saw her taking concrete steps to make it real. Now he needed clarity about why he hadn't been paying attention, what he truly wanted in the situation, and how he could communicate his real preferences to Sarah.

"Listen," I told him. "If you thought the plan was a definite no-go, say she wanted to open a B&B in Antarctica, you would've said 'no way' long ago and put an end to it. But that's not the case, so what's going on?"

The first question to ask if you've been using the Unconscious Yes is *why* you've been so checked out.

Is it because you don't care? Is it because you're so taken by your partner's enthusiasm that your default mode is to go along? Did you think the idea would just blow over? Or have you been so wrapped up in yourself that you've stopped paying attention to the other person? There are as many reasons as there are people and situations. What are yours? "I have to admit that I thought this would just go away," Ed said. "Or maybe I hoped it would. And I didn't want to pop her balloon—she gets so excited about this stuff."

"So now that it's looking serious, what's your fear, your biggest fear?" I asked.

"Lots of things," he said. "I don't want to annihilate the relationship by saying the wrong thing—she means everything to me. She'll probably hate me if she thinks I've been stringing her along. But baking cookies in Oregon? I can't do that. And what if we sink a ton of time and money into this, uproot our lives and then reality sets in and she's over it in ten minutes?"

Before you think about talking to the other person, you'll need to put your unspoken truths on the table for yourself and identify the realities and concerns you want to bring into the conversation. As I've been repeating, you can't connect with someone else before you connect with yourself.

Once you do that, you can take the next step: Homing in on

what you really want to tell the other person. What is the honest conversation you most want to have, and what's the most important thing for the other person to know?

"I guess the big thing is that I want her to know she's the most important thing to me, and that I have a lot of concerns about where this is all going," Ed said. "I don't want to shut her down. I want to find out what she's really got in mind when she thinks about this B&B thing. She knows me well enough to know I'll go nuts or feel trapped if I'm supposed to be some kind of housekeeper. Fire up the barbecue? Sure. Build something? No problem. But muffins? Really?

"Bottom line, I have to find a way to talk to my wife and tell her what I really think, especially that I have doubts. Not about us, but about this plan."

"So let's be specific: What's your objective here?" I asked.

Checking in with someone after you've been seriously checked out is about opening a door to communication. It may have nothing to do with getting immediately to the resolution of a problem. As I put it to Ed, the question is: How can I restart some honest communication around the issue and have the best outcome, even with bumps? If you and the other party love and/or respect each other, you will be able to sit and listen to each other's truth. That doesn't mean no one will be disappointed or hurt, but you can listen, and move closer to genuine understanding. You may find that you're not that far apart.

The goal of your inner work is to begin identifying and addressing the fears that have been standing in the way of making your "yes" (or "no") conscious, and fully expressed. Like Ed, you may have a list of fears and assumptions about what the other person thinks or plans. Opening a dialog will let you test those assumptions in the only way that works: by asking.

NEXT STEP: A CONNECTED CONVERSATION

How do you start a conversation like this? That's generally people's biggest concern, and Ed was no exception. "Never start by making the other person wrong," I told him, "or suggest that the problem is all about them. Start with where *you* are. If you have questions about what Sarah is thinking, put them out there. Her answers will give you new information, and may address your concerns."

Another important basic: Don't take for granted that the other person knows your positive feelings about them. Express them up front. It will remind both of you of why you want to be connected.

With some coaching from me, Ed decided to take the conversation this way: "Honey, I know you've been talking about that B&B for a long time, and I love you so much, I've been enjoying your excitement. Now it seems like this is getting real, and I want to check in and see where you are with everything. You always have plans for me, and I want to be sure I'm clear about what you have in mind."

If Sarah said something like, "We'll probably want to do some building and remodeling on the site, no matter where we wind up, so I thought you'd be in charge of that, and keeping the place in good shape," Ed's muffin concerns would be moot, and he could steer toward any other concerns he wanted to bring into the light.

No matter what she said, he could follow up with his own questions, and also express his concerns by saying, "Let me tell you where I am with all this."

Ed knew that he wanted to let Sarah know about his fear that the B&B would be another passing phase. So he practiced what he wanted to say. It sounded something like this: "You know I'd follow you anywhere. I didn't mind going to Hawaii and climbing a volcano because I knew we'd be coming back here. But this is different. This is our future. So I really want to be sure this is for us. I know we've stayed in B&Bs, but that's different than running one. I'd feel better if you'd think about going to work with some people at a B&B for a month or so before we go all-in. I could take a little time off and go check it out myself."

For Ed, and for most people, finding the words wasn't a problem once he had identified his fears and realized it was legitimate to talk about them. I often work with attorneys, people who have difficult conversations for a living, and when they first face the idea of talking to a loved one to drag an Unconscious Yes into the light, all of them struggle with what to say. But when we work out what the Unconscious Yes has really been about, and what the real fears and concerns are, the words flow. Fear is like a cloud bank. If you're in a plane flying above it—or when you step outside it and begin to analyze it—you can see its distinct shape and start understanding it. But when you avoid confronting it, you sink into a swirling fog, the same thing that happens when the plane descends into those clouds. You can't see your way forward, you can't find the words you need, and you can't connect.

Sarah was miffed when she realized that Ed had so many reservations about her plans, which she thought he'd signed on to. But they're talking now, and Ed is looking into the possibility of taking his contracting business to Oregon. Nothing's been decided, but the conversations have gotten real. And you can see the relief all over Ed's face.

Try it yourself: Dealing with the Unconscious Yes

Do you have an Unconscious Yes that's standing between you and an authentic connection with a loved one, friend, or colleague? Here's a recap of the questions you should ask yourself to move toward more genuine communication:

- Why have you allowed the issue to drift without your full attention?

- What are your biggest fears about dealing directly with the other person and telling them what you honestly think and feel?

- What is the honest conversation you most want to have, and what's the most important thing for the other person to know?

- What will your objective be in that conversation?

— What do you want to say? What positive feelings do you want to share? What questions do you have for the other person? What concerns do you need to express?

If you feel stuck, talking through the situation with a friend or a coach who can help you practice may make you feel more comfortable. You needn't feel as though you have to stumble through a tough conversation. It's fine to practice in the car until the words you want to say feel comfortable in your mouth.

And you don't have to do everything at once. Start small. Have one honest conversation about one small thing you've been avoiding by yessing it along. Things will get easier as you go.

TOOLS FOR THE ROAD

I'd like you to keep your focus on the two major exercises in this chapter, using the Four Rs (Regret, Resentment, Respect and Requests) to get clarity and move forward in a conflict, and identifying any Unconscious Yesses operating in your relationship.

If you skipped the tools at the end of chapter One, or would like to revisit them with a relationship focus, they'll support you in staying authentic with the people you care about.

CHAPTER 3

The New Knowing Grid

It would be easy to connect with yourself and move forward if connection were a matter of pure logic. You'd ask yourself what you wanted, make a clear decision to head that direction, and then just go.

But humans are complicated, and so are our feelings, memories, and inner worlds. As you look toward the future you want, your view may be clouded by expectations and emotions that come to you from other people and your own past. Those beliefs and feelings can keep you from seeing the possibilities available to you in this moment, and they can stand in the way of clear decision-making, ease, and connection. Received wisdom about "what always works" may be wrong. You may shy away from a choice that's right for you now because you tried it before and failed. Strong feelings like fear, shame, anger, regret, and resentment can push you to close down, rather than staying open to what you want and what can happen now.

Adding even more confusion, we play many different roles in life, each of which gives us different priorities and protects its own separate interests. The parent part of your heart and brain may want something very different from the entrepreneur, the spouse, and the lawyer parts of you, even though they all have the same face, live in the same body, and go by the same name.

At any given moment, you may be filtering reality through a whole collection of lenses, sometimes consciously and sometimes without any awareness at all.

That's why it can be so tough to answer the simple-seeming question "What do I really want?" or to see new ways forward from a stuck situation. Which "I"s are we talking about? And which ones can help you make the most authentic choices in a given situation? Who gets to make the call about which way to go? You have a choice about that, though it's easy to forget when you're experiencing the different parts of yourself as a cacophony in your head.

This chapter, the last part of this section on connecting with yourself, will walk you through a process designed to help you stay open and in the present as you make decisions. The first step in being open is to become aware of the filters you put between yourself and the decisions you need to make, or the people you want to connect with. When you see them, you're in a position to put aside the ones that don't serve you, cutting through confusion and clearing away old emotions. Then you can choose the perspective you most need to move through a problem or chart a new course. When you are clear about how you feel, what you know and what you want, the way is clear for making strong, authentic connections with the people and choices in your life.

MEET THE "NEW KNOWING" GRID

Do you stay or do you go? Start a new business or stick to what you've always done? Buy or rent? Send the kids to private school or public? Propose to your partner or break up?

Each of these questions requires you to imagine the new future you want to move into, and get your head and heart headed in the same direction. We make dozens of decisions a day, and we're supposed to be good at it. But after coaching scores of people through hundreds of important choices, I realized that most of them were trying to move forward and create something new for themselves without being clear about the filters that were keeping them from being truly open to the best solutions.

So I created a tool—a guide to help you first clear the way for whatever you want to bring into your life, and then make choices based on a clear connection to your authentic self.

I call the tool the New Knowing Grid, because it's designed to lead you toward a new understanding—new *knowing*—of what you want, and what you need, from yourself and others, to get it. It will bring you fully into the present, the best place to stand when you're making a decision.

The Grid, which you'll see on the following pages, takes you down four distinct tracks:

- The first column, labeled "Removing," walks you through the process of becoming aware of the emotions and expectations you bring with you from the past. The "removing" label refers to the last step: temporarily setting those filters aside.

- The second column, labeled "Assessing," helps you become aware of your usual way of listening and seeing, so you can decide if it serves you or gets in your way.

- The third column, labeled "Imagining," asks you to hold your new openness inside you and think not only about what you want, but also about what parts of yourself will help you do that.

- The final column, labeled "Going Forward," helps you decide how you want to carry what you've imagined into the world, and identify the partners, goals, and ways of being that will take you there.

REMOVING	ASSESSING
REMOVE ANYTHING WITH SHAME OR STRUGGLE ATTACHED – What kinds of emotions do you have in this situation? – Are any strongly negative? – What exterior factors bother or concern you?	**LEAVE OUT THE THINGS YOU CAN COUNT ON,** especially positive things or people, family, and friends.
REMOVE DEFEATS AND BAD MEMORIES – What feelings or assumptions do you carry from the past? – What memories is this situation bringing up? – Are fears or resentments coming up? – What do these old feelings take away from you now?	**OLD LISTENING** – We are many listeners. Which one will serve you best? – Do you listen from anger? – Do you listen from fear? – Do you listen from shame?
BAD FEELINGS / SENSITIVITIES – Are they based in fear or resentment? – What do they take away from you? – Forget what is not forgiven.	**OLD VISION / SEEING** – Do you have a strong vision of something that won't serve you moving forward?
WHAT CAN'T YOU LEAVE OUT? – What must you have as you move forward?	**OLD KNOWLEDGE** – Does it serve you? Or get in the way?
CHALLENGES – Things that make you hesitate or stop. – What *can* I control?	**WHICH <u>YOU</u> DO YOU TRUST?** – Of the many listeners we are, what are the odds that one great ability gets in the way of another?

IMAGINING	GOING FORWARD
CREATE AN OPENING	**CLARITY** – What do I know that I want to use to help me on my path?
NEW LISTENING – What is in this New Listening that you want to hear? – Who do you want to listen as (Mom, Dad, husband, wife, boss, employee, customer, friend, therapist, diabetic, business owner)?	**GOOD FEELINGS / POSITIVE SENSITIVITIES / EMOTIONAL ASSETS** – In this new situation, how do you want to feel? – What strengths will you draw on? – Who do you want to be? – What sensitivities will best serve you?
NEW VISION – In this New Vision, what do you want to see? – What do you have a strong vision of? – What do you want to create?	**ALLIES** – Who will walk this path with you?
NEW KNOWING – What do you want to learn or become aware of through this new knowing?	**GOALS** – What do you have to offer the world? – What will the impact or outcome be once your goal is reached? – What do you need?
YOUR AUTHENTIC SELF – Name all the parts of you that you want on this journey.	**ACTION PLAN** – What will I need to implement my plan? – What will be my first step forward?

In this chapter, I'll walk you through one complete situation in which we make the journey from confusion to clarity. I'm using a hypothetical case for this one, so I can go into detail without violating any clients' privacy, but the exchanges are closely based on the ones I have every day using this process.

As you look at the steps I'll describe, keep in mind that you can make this very simple, and use any question on the Grid to gain openness that will take you closer to an authentic connection with yourself. But you can get to know the process best if you pick a thorny situation in your life and walk it through the whole Grid.

You can get an overview by reading through the boxed questions in each section.

MARIA'S DECISION: SHOULD NINE-YEAR-OLD NICK PLAY FOOTBALL?

Maria is a busy young pediatrician and mom whose nine-year-old son Nick has been badgering her to let him join the local Pop Warner football team. Nick, she says, has always loved sports, and he seems happiest when he's got a ball in his hands—especially a football. When he's out at the park with his friends, he looks like he's in his element. But the family doesn't live near the park, and Nick can't play as much as he'd like to. He's begging to be allowed to play.

Maria is torn. She wants him to be happy, but she's worried he'll get hurt. She's leaning toward a firm no, "But it'll break his heart. I don't know what to do," she says miserably.

We used the Grid to dig below the surface and look at the issues in play.

STEP ONE: REMOVING OLD FILTERS. Identify the troubling emotions connected to the situation, and temporarily remove them from your decision-making.

With the outlines of the problem in mind, we began by wading into the realm of feelings to find emotional hotspots that might be shaping Maria's thinking. "When you think about Nick playing football, what sort of feelings do you have inside that you'd like to remove?" I asked her. "What feelings or concerns are making you the most uncomfortable?"

"You mean, what feelings do I have that are keeping me awake at night? I'm just so worried about Nick. I deal with a lot of parents, so I know it's common to worry. I don't want to be overprotective, but I have to be responsible. I have this image of him in casts and bandages that I'd really like to get out of my head...."

In this information-gathering stage, I also ask what she'd like to change in her outer world that's related to the situation.

"I don't like where we live—it's such a busy street and there's no safe place for the kids to play. That's one thing, and I hope it doesn't seem too random. The other thing is this: I feel like Tom, my husband, is putting me on the spot. If I could change anything, I'd get more support from him in making the hard decisions with Nicky. I feel like I'm in this all by myself, and I'm the bad guy who's going to say 'no' and make Nick hate me, if it comes to that."

As you note what you want to remove, you'll also get a glimpse of what you want. For Maria, that includes less worry about her son, a safer place for him to play, and better communication/support from Tom. You'll likely arrive at a number of concrete things you want in your situation at this point, so write them down.

What's Haunting You?

The next step down this path is to dig beneath the concerns that have come up. Fears and concerns don't come out of nowhere, and often, they're directly connected to experience. So looking at Maria's worries about Nick, I have to ask: What's up with that? Where do you think that concern came from? What's made you so sensitive to this?

This isn't deep therapy, and you don't need to delve into the hidden past. You'll probably get the answer you need by scanning your memory with those questions in mind.

"Well you can't miss those stories in the paper about the NFL guys getting brain injuries. That's my nightmare. You can't just throw a little kid onto the field and think he's going to come out fine. My brother broke his leg playing football in high school, and I went to a pro game where I actually heard someone's bone snap. It was horrific."

Make a list of the hot-button memories that spring to mind when you think about the situation at hand, as well as the factors—conversations, things you've read and heard—that make it feel especially sensitive.

Going deeper, we look at the sensitivities and bad feelings that arise around the situation. Sometimes, you'll find that you've been talking about these feelings all along, or sometimes the questions here will turn up something new.

For Maria, this stop on the Grid is a recap. "That fear of not being able to live with myself if Nick got hurt is what it all comes down to," she says. "I'm a doctor. I'm supposed to not wimp out when I have to make a tough decision about my own kid's health. As far as resentments, I just have that little bit of resentment toward Tom for leaving this all to me. Of course, I haven't exactly let him in since I've been such a control freak about it...."

What bad feelings do you notice? How much fear and resentment do you see? Write down your findings.

Looking at your "must-haves"

We change gears in the next square on the Grid, and I ask people to tell me about the things they can't do without as they make their decision. The question on the table here is: "What are the things you can't leave out?"

It's a wide-open question, I know, and I encourage people to list whatever comes to mind, whether it is inside them or on the outside.

"Okaaay," Maria says, hesitating. "Well, what I really want is watertight certainty about this issue. I'm not going to be frivolous or make a half-baked decision about something so important. I'm reading everything I can get my hands on, and I'm just going to try to look at the facts without letting emotion get in the way too much. I hate parents who let their kids run the show—kids aren't mini-adults! So I know I bend over backwards sometimes to prove I'm not a pushover, but that's me, and I can't leave it out."

The grid works to show you what's floating in your head and to help you make connections you might not make otherwise. So just write down whatever comes up when you ask yourself: What factors must I have in place before I can go forward?

I often find that asking people what they absolutely must have in a situation reveals not just desires but fears that are influencing or running the show. You may also find a perfectionist streak that's throwing a roadblock in your way. Maria's wording is a tipoff: "Watertight certainty" isn't possible. The must-haves on people's "can't leave out" list are sometimes extremely high hurdles to moving forward: "I must have an advanced degree before I can start thinking about changing careers." "I must have X amount of money before I can start working on my new business." "I must have 100 percent support from my family before I go on." I encourage clients to look carefully at what's on their must-have list to filter out the items that may be acting as reasons to delay facing or taking a big risk.

Maria and I would want to talk more, too, about her desire to keep emotion out of the decision-making process. Many smart people want to let their intellects dominate—especially in a situation where everyone's emotions are running high. But there's no avoiding the fact that emotion connects us to the authentic self—we need to allow in and examine the wisdom of our feelings. Your intellect wants you to make the best decision. And you can only do that by factoring in—and *listening to*—your emotions.

WHAT TRIPS YOU UP AND STOPS YOU?

The final stop in the Removing column: a list of challenges, the things that cause you to hesitate or stop altogether as you sort through what you want in this situation. Is there something that you can't get past when you try to move forward?

Maria concluded, "The thing that comes up for me again and

again is that I'm a *doctor,* and I just can't be a bad example for the people in our community. If I let Nick play, and that encourages other people to let their kids play and then they all wind up with brain injuries—I don't want that on my hands. But I don't want to be overbearing and crazy, either, as Tom thinks I am. I feel like there's a big 'No Way!' in my head, but then I see Nick in my mind's eye and how much he loves that stupid game. I don't know what to do, so I've been pushing this off as long as I can, and getting more and more stressed out."

The challenges you see could look like concerns about your resources or skills, other people's reactions, or conflicting agendas. Though they're not always fear-based, they're *often* "what ifs" and fears: "I've never done this before and I don't know how." "Where will I get the money?" "What if it doesn't work out?" "What will people think of me if X happens?" "What if people don't love/respect me anymore if I do this?" "I'm not smart/rich/young/brave/experienced/well-connected enough." "I know X will go ballistic."

Start by listing the big challenges—the things that stop you cold. Then list the factors that make you hesitate. It's okay to pour them all out at once and sort them when you're done. Finally, list the things you believe you can control. When I ask people to do this, I leave the idea of "what you can control" open-ended.

"The thing that lets me sleep at night," Maria says, "is that I know that when push comes to shove, I have control over what Nicky does and to a certain extent over Tom. If it comes down to I can't live with myself if I let Nick play football, then I can keep him out of the game. I'm the mom, I'm the doctor, and I know I have the ultimate say."

Your answers to this question are a window into what's giving you a sense of security, even power, in the situation. That sense of security may be rooted in something quite positive—for instance, maybe you know you have some control over the hours you put into your family life, and you can rearrange your schedule. You're the boss of you.

But sometimes, there's a sense of arrogance in the answers to

"What can you control?" When I'm listening to clients, I have an ear out for comments that show an inflated sense of importance— "I'm in control of X because I'm the boss and therefore I get my way." "I can control other people's responses because I am right/older/charismatic/more important than they are." Statements like this are telling, because arrogance is always a cover for insecurity (fear), and fear blocks the connection between you and your authentic self.

Maria's answer would lead us to a conversation about control. Some people feel acute discomfort when they sense they're not in the driver's seat and might not get their way. For our immediate diagnostic purposes, it's good simply to know if you need to watch for and be prepared to work with a tendency to be controlling.

NOW PUSH IT ALL AWAY

What you've created so far is a list of factors that are getting in the way of reaching a decision that reflects your authentic self. It's common to look at your collection of concerns, fears, sensitivities, and confusion and feel a little overwhelmed. Some people get all the way to the end of the Removing column and want to stop. But keep going—because the final task on this track is for you to temporarily push these feelings and concerns out of the way. Packing them into a mental storeroom that you can return to later if you want to retrieve anything.

Now the mental space in front of you is a little clearer.

STEP 2: ASSESS. Identify the ways you currently listen, see, and know what's going on in this situation.

As we move to the next column on the grid, labeled Assessing, we'll be conjuring up your situation again to make visible the way you generally use your senses to understand your situation—habits that may be unconscious until you turn the spotlight on them here.

There's one more bit of removing to do before we get on with this, though. I'd like you to make a list of all the positive factors or people you can count on to support you—the elements that constitute your safety net.

"That's my parents for sure," Maria says. "My father's a doctor too, and he'll definitely back me up. He and Mom are super-protective of Nick, their only male grandson. They'd probably offer to give Nick money or a Playstation or something if only he'd give up on the rough and tumble stuff. And my girlfriends are supportive. They're dealing with this same thing with their kids."

We believe that safety nets are only beneficial; they are resources that can help us bounce back if things go awry or bolster our confidence when we get shaky. But I often find that they can "protect" you from your real feelings, blunting legitimate fears and exerting subtle pressure on your decision-making. The same wonderful people you count on to help you in a pinch may expect—even if they don't say so—that you will repay their support by staying in line with their wishes. That financial backer you know will step in if you falter may have his own plans for your dream project. In that situation, it's easy to begin compromising and making decisions that grow less from true choice than from wanting to keep your "safety net" happy.

"So for right now, it's just you and your decision, alone together," I tell Maria. The safety net goes into the storeroom.

HOW ARE YOU LISTENING?

Now you can use the senses as a vehicle for identifying other filters that are coloring your decision-making. Let's start with hearing.

As you're listening to other people for advice, and considering your many sources of input and information about your decision, what part of you is listening? As I mentioned at the outset, each of us plays many roles, and in each of them, we have distinct interests and priorities. The lawyers I work with are often entrepreneurs who want to grow their businesses, and it's always illuminating for them to determine which part is dominant when they're making decisions. Is it the lawyer, who's attuned to potential difficulties and reasons for caution, or the gung-ho entrepreneur, who's full of enthusiasm and forward momentum? It's often the entrepreneur part of the person that calls me in to help break through blocks in the process, while the lawyer part hangs back, skeptical. When you don't know which part of you is listening, and which "ear" is in charge, you may find yourself in an invisible tug-of-war that leaves you stuck in an impasse.

In Maria's case, the conflict is between her professional doctor identity and her role as a mother: "I'm listening as a doctor, mostly, and as a person who has a responsibility to model good choices for other parents."

"What does that mean you listen for?" I ask.

"I definitely have an ear out for the reports on brain damage and kids hurt in sports. I'm on a few newsgroups of people who post the latest stories, so I don't miss much, whether it's on TV or in some paper or journal."

"And what emotion would you say you're listening through?"

"Concern. Fear. Maybe a little anger at the system that lets these injuries keep happening."

"What about other parts of yourself, like the mom part?"

"That's the squishy part," she says. "I guess the mom part gets steamrolled a little by the doctor. The mom is the part that feels guilty when she sees Nicky look so happy and wants to find a way to make this football stuff okay. But I've got all these facts running around my head and I can't see how that is even possible."

I ask which part she thinks will serve her best as she makes her decision.

"I wasn't even going to let the mom be a factor in all this, but as I talk about it, I think I need to, at least for the sake of discussion. It sounds almost crazy, but I wonder if there's another side to this. If I listened as Mom, I wonder what I'd hear, maybe something I've been missing. I want to tell you right now that the doctor part says this is outrageous, but I have this niggling feeling that she's leaving too much out."

When you think about what parts of you have been listening, ask yourself if you've excluded any significant parts of yourself, and if you've been filtering your listening through limiting emotions like anger, shame, or fear.

There are a couple of other kinds of old listening that I'd like to point out. You may be listening to familiar voices in your head that belong to others, to the past, or to self-talk and limiting beliefs that play in the background unnoticed. One way to get at them is to tune in to who's speaking loudly in your mind. When you're trying to create a new business, it might be the voices of colleagues who say, "You can't leave your old job! It's steady and you've got insurance!" If you're trying to break out of workaholic patterns and devote more time to yourself, it could be an ancient parental voice saying, "Sit here until your homework is done or you're in big trouble!" It might be your own voice saying, "Compared to [whoever], I don't have what it takes."

I frequently work with businesspeople who've experienced breakdowns in their plans, and gone through bankruptcies. They hold onto the fear and shame of failure, not simply saying "What can I learn from what happened?" but holding themselves back with voices that say, "I'm not going to let that happen to me again. I can't forgive myself for what went wrong."

What would happen if you tuned out the familiar voices in your head and listened for the quiet voice of your authentic self? What would happen if you listened through hope or confidence or love instead of fear? For this exercise, suspend your disbelief and see what happens. Our goal is to open up new possibilities, and old exterior voices are getting in the way.

WHAT ARE YOU SEEING?

Vision is an especially powerful sense as we imagine our possibilities. Outdated visions, as well as those rooted in limiting emotions, can stand like the false fronts of a town on a stage set, looking real, but serving only to block the view of many other options. Your old visions and ways of seeing can give you absolute certainty about what's reasonable and possible—and they can absolutely blind you to anything new. As an oft-quoted line puts it so well: "We don't see things as they are. We see them as *we* are." (*This saying has been used by Anaïs Nin, H. M. Tomlinson, Steven Covey, and others. However, its origin is not known*).

A strong vision of disaster, embarrassment, or someone "getting the best of you" may be keeping you from imagining an equally plausible outcome that would serve you better. You could be looking at a new relationship and seeing an old one that went wrong. You may be seeing a hated old boss as you hear the voice of a new employee. If your visions of your situation are superimposed with negative images or emotions, consider the possibility that they are getting in your way.

Maria's sharpest, most deeply held vision has nothing to do with Nick playing football safely. It is of him lying motionless on the ground with a concussion, or bandaged up with broken bones. "And you're right, that blots out everything else," she says. "Maybe I need to see something bigger."

Don't rule out the possibility that some vision from the past could also embolden you. If you look around your current office, with its rows of desks and people, and can still see your first office—just you, a desk, and a telephone—the old vision may give you a sense of accomplishment and pride. If that feeds you, enjoy it. If what you envision somehow holds you back, though, let go.

WHAT KNOWLEDGE DO YOU CARRY IN FROM THE PAST?

Your old listening and old vision combine with the rest of your history to contribute to a set of conclusions—your old knowledge. It's said that past is prologue, and that's true. But when lessons from the past dictate solutions that may not fit the present, the past is prologue only to more of the same.

Maria knows that "football is bad, it hurts you, and it's not for my kid." She also knows, "I'm a doctor. I can't let Nick play because I have to be super-responsible—other people are watching me." This old knowledge, she sees, is getting in the way of any other conclusion.

If what you "know" is that business is risky because your father started a venture that failed, or that there's no choice but the way things have always been done, or that Person X won't be responsive to you because "I never impress people like that," you're closing off the alternative paths that could lead to different outcomes.

Old knowledge can give us an advantage—an attorney who has extensive experience with certain kinds of cases can often leverage that to work more efficiently. But *only* if she can remain open to what's real right now, and what's unique about each new situation. If you walk into a training session and are 100 percent wedded to techniques you already know and use, the odds are vanishingly low that you'll pick up any new magic.

Old knowledge leads to old conclusions, and comfortable though that can be, it puts you in a box. You may have seen the same things twenty times before and believe your understanding is rock solid, but don't let that keep you from being aware and present. Look and listen as if for the first time, tapping the perspective of a new, curious part of yourself.

WHICH <u>YOU</u> DO YOU TRUST?

Going forward, you'll probably want to call on parts of yourself that haven't been active in your internal discussions. Visualize your inner self as a committee and think of inviting in the parts that have been overshadowed, drowned out or undervalued. Muzzling those parts creates the kind of polarization Maria felt as her doctor side overrode the compassion for her son she felt as Mom.

When you ask yourself, "Which parts of me are keeping this situation stalled? Which parts are saying, 'This is black and white—there's no need for discussion?'" you'll probably be able to put your finger on the parts of you that are holding you back.

"Here's the thing that's jumping out at me," Maria says. "All this fear I have is all about *me*. What people will say about *me*. How *I'll* feel if any kid gets so much as a bruise in a football game. It's the 'professional, watch your reputation' me talking. But I've hardly brought Nick into the conversation. The mom part of me is saying, 'My kid's happiness is at least as important as my fear.' And that's the part I think I need to trust and listen to for a while. I'll always be a professional, a doctor, too, but I can't let them bully Nick."

Memories, visions, and inner voices dominated by fear are almost ubiquitous, so don't be surprised or alarmed if you find that they play a big role in your old knowledge. Keep asking: Which part of yourself do you trust the most? What does it have to say? What comes first, the fear or a new way of experiencing your situation?

GOOD NEWS: THE GOING IS ABOUT TO GET EASIER

I know I've asked you to do a lot of work, and you may feel as though you've just climbed a mountain. But keep going—you're closing in on the payoff.

The questions you've answered so far have likely made you aware of feelings, memories, concerns, and parts of yourself that you haven't looked at side by side before. If you're like most of my clients, you have notes—lots of notes. Take some time now to review them. What do you see now? What's becoming clear to you?

STEP 3. IMAGINE SOMETHING NEW. Let the best parts of yourself envision the possibilities.

This part of the grid is devoted to fresh possibilities.

You can create an opening for something new simply by standing in this moment, unburdened by the negative or outdated emotions, memories, and habits that you've discovered. The view is different from here. Think about what you'd like to do moving forward. At this point, people can frame their big questions in a different way, and open themselves to different decisions than the ones they were considering walking in.

For Maria, the question becomes: If I were the mother I wanted to be when it comes to this decision, what would I conclude about letting Nick play football? If I weren't so certain that there's no safe way to play this game and that I need to take the blame for every injury, what might I learn and consider?

"That shifts the whole discussion," Maria says. "I'd be figuring out what people know about keeping the game safe for kids, and looking for programs that emphasize that. Even if it's Nerf balls and padded gym space. The big thing is, I wonder now if there's a way for him to play that's not brutal, so he can get the benefit of doing what he loves, and I can give him that gift."

Stand in that clearing in your mind and ask: *If I were the person I want to be in this situation, operating from the part of myself I trust the most, what would I do?* When I'm coaching, I encourage people to think out loud. You can talk to a recorder and listen back. You might also want to write down your thoughts, or kick things around with a friend or coach.

FLESHING OUT YOUR SCENARIO, WHAT WOULD YOU LIKE TO HEAR AND SEE?

Stand in the future. What changes would you like to see rippling into your environment as a result of your decision? Engage your senses to give you a three-dimensional sense of what your new scenario feels like. Start with sound, particularly what you hear people saying as you interact with them in this new reality. Be mindful of which You will be listening. Enlist the part or parts of yourself that will serve you best.

Now imagine those parts listening to the sounds and voices of what you most want to hear in your new, resolved situation. What are the important people in the situation saying? What are you hearing in your environment, from friends, media, and the wider circle connected to the situation?

"I'm listening as a mom first, and also as a doctor," Maria says. "I want to hear my son saying things like, 'Mom, I love this! I just had the best day of my life!' I want to hear the announcer say Nick just scored a touchdown, and I want to hear a crowd cheering for him. I want to hear his coach say that Nick is the natural leader I know he is. I want Tom to come home and tell me that he went to watch the kids practice and talked to the coach, and found out all this great information about how they're teaching kids to tackle in new ways to keep them from getting head injuries. I want to hear other moms talking about how good it was for their kids to be involved in sports like this, and I want to hear other kids on the team talking about how Nick is taking the lead in playing a safe game. Oh, and I want to hear about some great new helmet that's specially designed to prevent concussions in kids Nicky's age. Can't someone invent something like that?"

Now move to vision: What would you like to see around you in this new future? If you've been having a conflict with someone, maybe you'd like to see yourself laughing with him instead, or working closely on a deal. If you're dreaming of starting a new business from your home, maybe you'd like to see a couple of your friends sitting around your dining room table drinking coffee, joking around, and helping you pack boxes for shipping.

Maria's list is varied. "First and foremost, I want to see that huge smile on Nicky's face, and I'd love to see him hanging out with new friends. It would be thrilling to see a little trophy for his team, and to see Tom taking him out to toss a ball around. I just had this crazy idea that maybe I can gather up the research I'll be doing on 'safer football' and make a blog or something for moms who are wrestling with this stuff. There have to be a zillion of them, just counting my friends and patients. I can see the picture I want on the blog: Me smiling in my white coat and stethoscope, with my arm around Nick, who's in a football uniform. He has a big grin, and charcoal smeared under each eye."

What's your vision for your new course of action? What do you want to create? You may see a diploma on the wall or business cards with a new title. Maybe you see yourself in a new setting, or surrounded by different kinds of people. Maybe you're looking at a new baby, or a credit card statement with a zero balance, or a text from the person you've been dating that says, "I love you." Maybe you see your name in a news story announcing your new job or invention or Everest climb. What do you most want to *see* as a result of your decision?

YOUR NEW WAY OF KNOWING

What you take in with your newly focused senses will change the way you understand the situation. As you imagine yourself choosing a new direction, what do you want to know? What do you want to be true for you, with the changes you see yourself making? With all the old, outworn beliefs and memories pushed aside, what new knowledge will help and guide you?

"When I picture myself in this situation where I'm looking for ways to let Nick play, instead of ways to make my fear go away, this is what I hope I'll know," Maria says. "That I can't wrap Nick up in bubble wrap and protect him from everything, so there are going to be times he'll try things I'm nervous about—and we'll both live. I want to know I can make a decision for right now, and if I need to change it, I can. We're not really locked in for the rest of our lives, even if I act like it sometimes. I want to know I can trust Tom to help me figure out what's best for Nick, and that we'll both have to let Nicky into the discussion too—it's not about us imposing our will on him, but helping him be his own person. I want to know I can share what I learn with other moms. And I want to know that I don't let fear drive me. I can be a better mom if I'm not always paralyzed because I'm sure something bad is going to happen to Nick."

The most powerful knowledge connects with your new vision and how you want that vision to feel. Instead of being fear-based ("I want to know I cannot fail"), it looks like this: "I want to know that I've surrounded myself with people I trust, people who've got my back." "I want to know I'm pay attention to my gut feelings." "I want to know I'm not putting everyone else's dreams ahead of my own." "I want to know I'm going for it instead of letting fear hold me back." "I want to know I'm doing something that matters to me and other people." "I want to know I'm being kind as well as being a strong leader."

What "new knowing" do you want to have?

CHOOSE THE NEW TEAM YOU

Finally, look back over your list of which parts of you will be most helpful and trustworthy on this journey and create the inner "team" that will go forward. Maria's trusted parts emerged fairly early on the Grid: She wanted her mom side to help her lead from the heart, and consider ways Nick could either safely play ball or try a sport that would make him equally happy. She'd bring the doctor along, and tap her medical knowledge to give a critical eye to studies on preventing head injuries and making football safer for kids. She also thought she could use the help of the part of herself that likes to network with other moms, since she wanted to share what she learned.

What parts of you will give you the best, clearest, fear- and shame-free guidance? Write them down. That's your authentic self.

STEP 4: GO FORWARD WITH AN ACTION PLAN. Now you have a much sharper idea of who you've been and who you want to be in the situation. You've enlisted the most trustworthy part or parts of yourself and asked them to create a vision of what you want in your new situation, the one your decision is aimed at bringing into being.

You've also cleared away bad feelings, memories, and blocks from the past—a pile of emotional stuff that was blacking out possibilities almost before you could see them. Feel how different that is from simply scribbling down a list of pros and cons, or reaching for the most expedient way to put out a fire.

The action plan you'll make now will pull from everything you've learned to help you create what you've imagined. It's not the ultimate plan for all time, it's a plan that will help you move toward what you've decided you want right now, a plan you can change when you check in with yourself and find that your desires have shifted. Course corrections are inevitable, not a sign that you've failed. You're experimenting with a new way of being, and it will need adjusting. Think about your last eye exam. As the doctor put different prescriptions in front of you and asked, "Which is better, this or this?" sometimes it was hard to tell. Option A can blur into Option B. And that's not a terrible problem. Try, refine, see what gives you the most clarity.

The other thing I often tell clients—because it's true—is that you are Yoda. You are learning to be the master of your own energy. In *Star Wars* terms, the authentic self you have been using the Grid to reach is the positive side of the Force, the energy supply that will carry you toward happiness and connection with everything around you. It's worth the effort. To quote the Jedi master, "Patience you must have, my young padawan."

CLARITY, GOOD FEELINGS, AND ALLIES: LOOK BACK AT WHAT YOU'VE DISCOVERED

Go over the lists you made in the Imagining column—all you wanted to see, hear and know—and then step into the movie of what you want to experience and be in your new situation. Let scenes unfold in your mind as you experience the scenario you've created. Feel yourself moving through it, then watch it as though you're the audience.

Now, for the final column on the Grid, ask a series of questions:

What do I know now that I want to use to help me on my path?

As Maria consults her notes and mentally enters her future vision, she has new clarity: "The big thing I know is that I don't have to have all the answers myself. I can work with Nick and Tom to figure things out, and it'll make us a better family. I know they'll have fun, and it'll even be an adventure for us. I never thought about *that* before."

Your answers here may closely echo the ones that came up when you thought about what you want your "new knowing" to look like. That's fine. Pay attention to any gaps between the two lists.

How do I want to feel on this path? What are my emotional assets?

Replay your movie of the future. What emotions are you experiencing? What parts of your emotional being serve you best? For

Maria, the answers come almost instantaneously. "Less fear, more love. That sounds corny," she says with a smile, "but that's it for me. I think it'll make a lot of difference. Of course I love Nicky more than anything. But I don't know if it was coming through because of all my fears about myself and all those fears for him."

How do you want to feel? Your answer may be one, none, or many of these: Confident. Inspired. At peace. Relaxed, not angry. Optimistic. Centered. Clear. Hopeful. Loving. Close. Independent. Empowered. Open. Brave. Unburdened. Out from under. Happy. Free.

Who are my allies? Who will walk with me on this path?

Not everyone will follow you when you begin operating from your authentic self. Anyone who's been taking advantage of you, standing in your way, feeding your bad feelings about yourself, or benefiting from the status quo will probably feel challenged by your new choices. And you probably have a good sense of who will be at your side on this new path, and who may go. Ask your authentic self: Who are my allies?

Maria was relieved to be able to list Nick and Tom. "I'll have to see who is okay with me backing off being so militant," she says. "My parents will probably come around, and as I do research and share it, I'm sure some of the moms I know will—my closest friends, basically. Beyond that, we'll see."

Remember if you find anything that concerns you as you do this review, you can draw on the inner resources we've been uncovering—as well as the Grid process itself—as you move forward.

AND FINALLY, THE PLAN

At last, it's time to make a concrete plan for moving toward the situation you want. In the Imagining column, as you described what you'd like to see, hear, and know as a result of your decision, you were creating the basics of an action plan. Go back to those lists, and for each item ask: What is my next step for bringing this about?

Here's how it worked for Maria as she went through her "new listening" list.

Item: "I want to hear my son say, 'I just had the best day of my life!'" and "I want to hear the announcer say, 'Nick just scored a touchdown.'"

Action step: Start checking out the program with an eye to signing him up.

Item: "I want to hear his coach say, 'Nick is the natural leader I know he is.'"

Action step: Meet the coach and get details about the program. Ask him to watch Nick play?

Item: "I want Tom to come home and tell me that he went to watch the kids practice and talked to the coach, and found out all this great information about how they're teaching kids to tackle in new ways to keep them from getting head injuries." Bringing Tom into the picture requires talking to Tom about her change of heart.

Action steps: Talk to Tom about the football team. Ask if he'll go watch the kids play. Ask if he'll go with me to talk to the coach and staff about what they do to prevent injuries. Find out if there really are new ways to tackle or if that's just a fantasy.

You can continue in this way through all the lists you've made in the Imagining column, concretely asking: What do I need to do to create this?

Action steps in hand, you can prioritize.

First, ask: "What's one small thing I can do today to get started?"

Then put the steps in a logical order: What do I need to do next?

For Maria, talking to Tom, asking questions of the coaching staff, and doing research on safety were clear preliminaries, and she would work her way forward from there.

I'm not lingering over this part of the process, because you know how to make lists and set priorities. The problem has been that you likely did not know how to remove the blocks standing between you and your authentic self in order to connect with what the best parts of you really wanted.

Now you can.

As you set out toward your genuine goals, know that you can use the guideposts in the Going Forward column of the Grid to help keep you positive, focused, and open. The Imagining column and the "movie" you make of it will be a touchstone reminding you of what you set out to do.

What you have now is clarity. You know what you want. You have access to the best parts of yourself, unburdened by emotional baggage.

You are Yoda.

PART II

A Closer Look at Connection in Business

The basic rules of connection apply in every part of your life, and now that you've gotten the basics, I want to drill down and show you some specific applications.

In the next two chapters, I'll walk you through the way I teach my business clients—many of them entrepreneurs and professionals who run their own operations, large and small—to use the tools of connection to solve the problems they face.

These chapters are packed with the specific tools and techniques I use to dig below the surface symptoms of trouble and identify the human issues that can cloud business owners' perspective and keep them from connecting effectively with their clients, customers, and staff. In particular, we work with the emotions—hope, denial, fear, avoidance, and perfectionism, to name a few—that can have more impact than cash flow does on the success of a business.

The material you'll find here will guide you through the process of evaluating business situations, getting useful input, refining your plans, and making course corrections as you go.

These chapters are the equivalent of a "business consultation in a box," based on more than thirty years of business and coaching experience. They're a great basic template for creating an environment that's firing on all cylinders, driven by authenticity and connection.

I think you'll find the concepts here useful whether you're in business for yourself or trying to get any group of people working together successfully toward a common goal.

CHAPTER 4

Business Turnarounds: Creating Connection and Success in the Office

In the first section of the book, you experienced what it feels like to be connected to your authentic self. That puts you miles ahead when you turn your focus to solving problems in your business—because often, the biggest problems people face in the workplace reflect the confusion and lack of clarity they carry inside. Now that you know what *you* want to be doing (and not doing), you can think about what you want for your job or company.

You may have some clear ideas: Make more money. Find ways to grow. Work less (or more!). Have more satisfaction and peace of mind. People often hire me to consult in their businesses because they think they have the wrong staff in place, the wrong marketing, the wrong everything in their operations. They're focused almost entirely on factors outside themselves, and that's where they think their salvation lies.

But no matter what your industry or profession, and no matter what obstacles you face, the solutions depend on creating connection inside your business. This kind of connection starts with you, and flows from choices that allow—and require—authenticity from everyone involved, from the support staff to salespeople and executives. When you've got that, you can look around and see that you're surrounded by people doing the jobs they want to do, full of enthusiasm for their projects and the goals they want to reach.

When you are connected to your workplace, whether you own it or signed on to support it, you have a real sense of purpose. You care about the results of what you do every day. Your work matters to you and you're proud of it. You know that you are exactly where you're supposed to be. When you and those around you share that mindset, you will succeed—and so will the business as a whole. Because that kind of connection is everything.

If you are walking into this chapter without that level of connection, that all may sound impossible to achieve. Connecting with yourself is hard enough. Connecting a whole community of people and objectives may seem dauntingly complex.

But you will use the same combination of compassion and no-bull candor. Those will give you the power to, first, reveal what stands between you and authentic connection in your work life. And then, you can refine (or overhaul) how you connect with colleagues and employees, as well as customers and vendors—so that all of you can thrive.

TO START FROM WHERE YOU ARE, BE HONEST ABOUT WHERE YOU ARE

One of my specialties as a coach is business turnarounds, and I can tell you that every amazing turnaround starts with the truth—because authentic connection requires acknowledging and working with what really exists.

That sounds simple, but it's always interesting to see how much blindness sets in when we're in the realm of money and business. Many people fall into an avoidance game because our fears, and sometimes our sense of shame, about money are huge. The first response is often to look away rather than to dig beneath the surface of a scary or difficult reality.

So I'd like to start by telling you this: It's safe to look at any business problems you face, and it's safe to *see* what's going on. Frustrating situations and setbacks in your business are absolutely normal. Everyone I've ever met who has spent time in the business arena gets knocked down.

Falls, scrapes, and scrambles are a normal part of business evolution, not proof that you're in over your head. Taking hits is part of the game, and sometimes, you'll feel like you're on the ground with the wind knocked out of you. It can disorient you, and hurt like hell. But the lessons you learn by getting up and working through the rough patches are often the ones that let you make the greatest leaps. If things are tough, contentious, or chaotic right now, this chapter will help you understand why, so you can change them. If they're going well, I'll show you how to be sure you stay on course and improve.

Ignoring problems is common, in part because there's a widespread belief that if we focus on the craft or service we're offering, we can ignore the "business" part of business—managing, tracking, and growing it—because "it will take care of itself." (It's the classic problem of working *in* the business instead of *on* it.) That can work while an operation is small, but from the beginning, *someone* is always managing the business. If you're not taking an active role in setting the direction and tone, then your clients, employees—or chaos—will.

That leads to scenarios like these, which I often see in my coaching practice:

- The office where everyone is putting in eighty-hour weeks, and no one has stopped to notice they're not making a profit. "We're working so hard we must be making money," the employees and partners assume.

- The longtime business where the facilities have started to look shabby and customer service is sketchy at best, but everyone insists that business has slowed down because "the economy is so bad."

— The office with an elephant in the room: staff members who get their way because they're bringing in an outsized share of revenue, but are forcing decisions that undermine everyone else's relationships with clients. "It's killing the business, but we can't afford to make them mad," their colleagues and bosses say.

Such situations can seem impossibly stuck, but every one of them transforms when the principals realize they can make new choices that let them connect with the solutions that come from facing the truth.

In this chapter, I'll put the power of choice in your hands. I'll show you how to pull back and evaluate what's happening in your business so you can see not only the weaknesses that are undermining you, but also where your strengths and true resources lie. At that point, you can step in to repair what's broken. And you can build a foundation grounded in integrity and supported by a web of strong connections that link you and your staff to your mission, your customers, and each other.

An important note: As you do this work, pay attention to how you feel. If you're scrambling to solve problems, you may be overwhelmed, and you may not realize how stressed you are, or how much that affects your decision-making. Take things a step at a time. The work we do seems like it's all upstairs—in the mind—but it's important to be aware of your feelings and how you hold onto them.

The material in this chapter draws on my work with business owners and managers, but no matter what your title or where you stand in the chain of command, this chapter will give you the tools to understand how your work environment is functioning, and assess your place in it. If you're not a boss, this chapter will help you think like a good one, and see your workplace through your boss's eyes.

The working world is a microcosm of the wider world. So even if you don't have a business, I hope you'll stay with me. There's much value in learning how to go from traveling through the world on autopilot, as most of us often do, to looking, listening, and learning from what's really there.

If your business has a strong, connected infrastructure and you're on an authentic path, you can do anything you want—take your business in a new direction, try something new to grow—and even if your experiments don't work out, you'll be fine. A rock solid foundation will let you weather the knocks that lead to the greatest successes.

So let's start digging.

THE ONE-WORD TEST
FOR YOUR BUSINESS: INTEGRITY

When I walk into a business, my goal is to help people move past any problems and confusion on the surface to find the human truths that are driving them. I do that by looking for and testing the business's integrity—the force that holds it together and makes it more than a disjointed collection of people and projects. Where there is integrity, there can be connection, satisfaction, and success.

The Collins English Dictionary's definition of integrity comes at it from three distinct angles:

1. adherence to moral and ethical principles; soundness of moral character; honesty.

2. the state of being whole, entire or undiminished: *to preserve the integrity of the empire.*

3. a sound, unimpaired, or perfect condition: *the integrity of a ship's hull.*

In terms of your business, we're talking about whether you operate with honesty and reliability, whether all the parts and people on your team contribute to a strong whole, and how sound the enterprise is overall. As we take stock of each of these pieces, you'll see your business with a perspective that you may not have had before. Keep in mind that every new challenge or breakdown you spot offers you an opportunity to make changes that will finally address problems at the root. That's where the fun starts, and where turnarounds gain momentum. If you're looking for serious change, this is the time to say, "Bring it on."

THE STRUCTURAL INTEGRITY CHECK

I've been a boater for most of my life, and boating teaches you from the start that you have to pay attention to details. Before setting out, you check to see that the engine compartment has no fuel leaks, and the hull is free of cracks, holes, or rust spots that could let in water. Are ropes and lines in good condition? Do you smell heating or cooking fuel that might be leaking from a tank? Does the radio work? The navigation equipment? Have you run down a checklist of emergency gear to be sure you have it, and that it's in good condition?

Doing this check of survival necessities is crucial—you don't want to wind up discovering a problem when you're out to sea and have to call the Coast Guard, hoping you can stay afloat.

The stakes are just as high for your business. Having a strong structure, ensuring that essentials are in place, and having a procedure for spotting and correcting weaknesses can be the difference between sinking and floating.

LET'S START WITH THE WAY
YOU <u>THINK</u> THINGS ARE

Before we go through the integrity check together, I'd like you to collect your thoughts about what's going on in the business, what it needs, and where you're headed. In essence, I want you to take a snapshot from the captain's deck and give me your best assessment of where you are right now.

First, think about the big picture, the reason you're in business. Do you have a mission statement? You may be a law firm, say, but what's your purpose? What did you set out to do? Who in particular did you set out to help?

Then take stock of how things are going now, using the questions below. Some might take a simple yes or no, and some will require more. You can do this exercise in your head, but I encourage you to write down your answers, which will make them more useful later. Be as honest as you can.

How's the Business? Your Personal Survey

1. What is the number one challenge or priority in your business?
2. What do you think your employees would say are the biggest challenges?
   a. How different are their answers from yours?
   b. Have you addressed those challenges? How? Have your efforts succeeded?
3. If you have talented employees with great potential, do you have enough time to work with them personally to bring them up to the level that would best serve you both?
4. How much investment have you made in the infrastructure of your business?
   a. Do your employees have the tools to do their jobs?
   b. Do they agree with how you run your business?
   c. Do they know what's important to you as an employer and/or business owner?
   d. Are they really invested in how you want your business run, or do they just agree with you because they're afraid of losing their jobs?
5. How often do you check in with your staff? If there is an issue, how long would it take for you to hear about it? How would you find out?
6. Do you impart your knowledge to your employees? If so, how does that happen? If not, are you afraid of giving too much away, fearing they might leave and take your knowledge and the business with them?

7. Are there incentives for exceeding goals and expectations?
8. Other than monetarily, how do your employees know if they're moving in the right direction?
9. Do your employees have a voice in your business? If so, what value do you see in that for them and you? If not, why not? What do you think is getting in your way of allowing them that communication?
10. As an owner or manager, if you could have anything you wanted from your employees, what would it be? What would the optimal measurable result or achievement look like for the business?
11. If you are in a partnership, how do you divide responsibilities?
    a. Do you feel like you are both/all moving in the same direction?
    b. Do you have unresolved issues in the business? What are they? What could you accomplish if they were resolved?
12. What goals/milestones have you set for the business?
    a. Are you on track? How do you know?
    b. How did you get there?
    c. If you haven't, what would it take for you to reach those goals/milestones?
13. What are you most proud of in your business? What's working well? Why?

The questions are designed to get you thinking about how you position yourself, how you think you show up as a leader, employer, or manager, and what the effects are. I know the tendency is to put most of your energy into looking at what's broken, but as a coach, I often pay especially close attention to the answer to the last question, about what's working well, because it often contains problem-solving gold. Some business owners, to give you just one example, notice that particular operations run the most smoothly when they are not closely involved—or *only* when they're hands-on. They may initially be uncomfortable with that knowledge, but once they have the awareness, they can leverage it for the good of the business. Don't judge your answers. Just stay curious and open to what they tell you.

The inspection: What's been hiding in plain sight?

So far, you haven't even needed to get out of your chair on this fact-finding mission. But now I'd like you to take a walk around your workplace and do the equivalent of inspecting the hull of a boat for cracks. The "cracks" you'll look for are broken connections, and you can spot them by carefully paying attention to what's around you.

1. WHAT DO YOU SEE?

Look for messes. This isn't about being a neat freak. It's a fact of life that in an office, desktops may disappear under reams of paper and files may stack up. Sometimes that's because people are incredibly busy, but sometimes there's a problem—someone is ignoring the filing system, holding onto things he shouldn't, or sinking under a load she can't handle. Even in these days of the supposedly paperless office, one or two desks might look as though a cyclone hit, and I always ask why. And if I walk past a desk one day and see a stack of fifteen files, then notice the same files there two days later, I ask what's going on. Because a lasting mess is often a sign that something is broken.

A friend of mine owns a car-repair business. The quality of the work coming out of his shop is outstanding, and people go out of their way to get his team's expert touch. But he can't take his business to the next level by landing lucrative contracts with insurance companies. What's the problem? It's obvious to me when I drive into his place—which looks like a junkyard. The office is piled up with greasy parts, dusty papers and boxes, and there's no clean place for a customer to sit. The bathroom is unfit for humans.

All this is invisible to my friend, who insists that his high-quality work and great prices should speak for themselves. I agree, they should. But the mess is delivering another message: "I don't care about my clients' comfort, or their paperwork."

Where are your messes? What message are they sending?

Look for "I don't cares." There's an endless number of ways to tell clients, employees, vendors, and peers that you don't care about them, and thus give them reason to tune you out. Though these little insults are often small and cheap to remedy, they may linger for years, because it's easy to think they're "too minor" to pay attention to.

Take basic maintenance, for example. I'm on the road a lot, and I eat out regularly in a whole gamut of restaurants, from greasy spoons to five-star dining rooms. In every category, I've walked into disgusting, paper-strewn restrooms with sticky floors, blocked-up plumbing, and/or no soap or hot water. I know upkeep can be demanding. I know the front of the house may be gorgeous. But when I find that no one cares about the restrooms, I wonder what else isn't getting taken care of. That's the creeping doubt you plant with an "I don't care."

"I don't cares" can come in the form of typo-filled documents or phones answered by people who are hard for clients to understand. They can involve ushering a client into an office and making her wait while you stare into a screen, texting or typing. Not acknowledging a customer's presence, or email, or phone call. Interrupting a serious meeting with an employee to plan your kid's soccer game. Being a miser with courtesy and common sense. Making the face of your company—the people who deal with the public—your lowest paid, most inexperienced, least competent staffers, because "what does it take to answer the phone?" Putting a client on hold and never coming back.

What do you see when you walk through your business? How many ways is it saying, "I don't care?"

Look at screens. As you look into offices and pass desks, is everyone staring into a screen? Are people engaging with each other and clients, or are they distracted? At your team meetings, are staffers checking their devices, texting, or taking calls? Are they answering personal e-mail or surfing websites instead of focusing on the work?

Digital distractions are everywhere, and it's difficult to avoid them, but they can easily rob people of the ability to be fully present with their work and each other. Studies have shown that every time we're distracted, *it can take ten to twenty minutes to fully re-engage.* How well are people in your business connecting with the tasks in front of them? How often do they have to spend twenty minutes coming back from another distraction?

Remember that "multitasking" is an illusion. It really *isn't* possible to be with a client fully while texting or taking a call. With every glance down at a screen, human connection weakens. It might even break.

Have you managed to do your walk-through without checking your phone? What messages are coming through the screens around you?

Look at your financials. What's coming in and what's going out? This is a separate piece, requiring its own inspection, but I put it here because though it's obvious, it's often ignored. People think the accounting department has things covered. Bills are being paid, the lights are still on—it's all good, right? But take the time to get someone to explain exactly what the numbers look like, and what they mean. Physically looking at them yourself, asking about the process of managing the money, and looking for messes there, too, is a vital part of the process. If you've got this covered, great. If not, take a deep breath and schedule some time to dive in.

2. WHAT DO YOU HEAR?

Listen for emotions. As you stop by people's desks to chat, what do you hear in their voices and comments? Fear? Anger? Resentment? Skepticism? Confidence? When clients talk about your business, what do they say? What emotions do they convey?

Listen to what your customers hear. Call your business and experience how it comes across through the phone. I've worked with car dealerships that have $10-million to $15-million facilities and operating budgets of $1 million a month, but hire a minimum-wage receptionist to direct (or misdirect) calls. High-end conservative law firms have left me listening to static-y rock 'n' roll, with no idea if anyone would return. Or run me through a maze of push-button options, not one of which involved talking to a human.

What happens when a caller encounters your business by phone? If you're in a community where English is a second language for many, do you have bilingual employees fluent in both English and the dominant languages? My clients have been known to call this listening exercise picky, and you may think I'm harping on this phone thing—but the way you treat customers by phone, I've found, is a real tip-off to the way you treat them in person. And they know it. A system that regularly inconveniences or annoys them is a significant crack in your infrastructure.

THE "WHOLENESS" INTEGRITY CHECK: WHAT DO YOU PICK UP ABOUT THE ENERGY IN THE PLACE?

I sometimes get curious looks when I ask people to rate the energy in their business on a scale of one to ten, but most of them can easily tell when the atmosphere is happy, tense, fearful, or confident. What you're really looking for is engagement, because that's a hallmark of connection. Think back to the description of connection that opened the chapter. How much enthusiasm and sense of purpose, and how much commitment to the purpose of the business, do you feel from the people around you? Where is it the strongest? Where is the pulse faint?

What you find here is one good indication of how well individuals are rowing in the direction you want to be going, and how unified the business as a whole seems to be. That's the second definition of integrity.

People sometimes get upset and a little defensive when I first mention I'll be looking for integrity in their business, as if I'm questioning their honesty. Let's be honest: business can get nasty and complicated sometimes, but that's just the nature of the beast.

What I'm really talking about when I turn my attention to this variety of integrity is honor, the business of fulfilling obligations, keeping commitments and treating everyone—from the cleaning people to clients and rivals—with respect.

As you walk around your business and think about how things have been done, answer the following questions. They'll give you a good sense of how strong or weak your integrity is in the practice of your business.

1. DOES YOUR COMPANY RUN ON TIME? Do your meetings start and end when you say they will? Are there consequences for being late? Do your orders get delivered as promised? Do your invoices get paid when they're supposed to? Being on time can have a huge effect on your productivity, profitability, and employee morale.

2. DO YOU HONOR YOUR COMMITMENTS? If I polled your top customers right now, what would they say about your integrity and the way you meet commitments? Do your vendors and contractors get paid, or do you haggle over their invoices?

3. DO YOU MEAN WHAT YOU SAY AND SAY WHAT YOU MEAN? In the 1942 Dr. Seuss book *Horton Hatches the Egg*, Horton the cartoon elephant promises a mother bird that he'll sit on her egg until she returns from a much-needed vacation. Time passes, seasons change, and the task gets tedious, but Horton keeps his word. "I meant what I said / And I said what I meant," he remarks. "An elephant's faithful / One hundred per cent!" It's a simple story, but it's woven through with reminders to act with character and integrity.

How do you rate on the Horton scale? Do you and your employees hide or minimize problems when you communicate internally and with customers? Are you honest with yourself and others? Do you make realistic promises, or do you exaggerate what you can deliver? Do your salespeople have the customer's best interest in mind?

4. DO YOU SPREAD THE RESPECT AROUND? Do you treat your employees with as much consideration as you give your clients? It's devastating for employees to watch their bosses treat clients like gold, even as they treat their own workers and staff like trash.

SUM UP YOUR DISCOVERIES SO FAR

Pause now to reflect on what you've seen, good and bad. What you've observed has probably tempered your original impressions, and you probably feel ready to start taking action to address the issues you've noticed.

But don't do it yet. There's more fact-finding to do first.

TESTING YOUR REALITY AGAINST OTHER PEOPLE'S: THE EMPLOYEE SURVEY

The perspective and solutions you need won't just come from you. To underline the obvious, connection can't happen in isolation. Building it in your business means allowing yourself to contact other people's truths about what's going on, and that requires opening channels of communication, and quite possibly learning new ways to listen.

You can begin this process with a short survey that goes out to every employee. Its questions open the door to your office, and let people tell you what they need and want, as well as what they perceive as problems and solutions. You'll probably find out that you've missed picking up on crucial elements of what's going on in your business—and that may aggravate you. But each discovery is an opportunity, a chance to make a shift that benefits your business. *If people feel safe enough to be candid,* they'll tell you exactly why you're not getting what you want from them, and how you could.

The issue of safety is key. The purpose of the survey is to gather information, not to identify "complainers" so you can chop off their heads. It's imperative to make that clear, because if you don't, people will protect themselves by telling you only what you want to hear.

You can make the process feel safe, and encourage candor, by doing several things: Explain what you're doing and make clear that the purpose of the survey is to make people's experience at the company better, and to make the company better as a whole. If your business is large enough, offer people a chance to respond anonymously. Let them know that their communication with you won't be public, and that the only people who will see the completed surveys are you, your partners if you have any, and a coach if you're working with one. It's counterproductive for middle managers, directors, or anyone else to be involved.

Resolve to keep listening, especially when it gets painful, and to respect the opinion of everyone who responds. You may find that your survey respondents are the most insightful business analysts you've ever hired. Here's a suggested sample survey to help you get started.

[Our Company's] Employee Survey

The objective of this survey is to let you tell us how you see [Our Company] and to get your thoughts about how we can all make this business even better. I will personally go over all the surveys received. I see this as a great opportunity for honest communication and to address the challenges that you and the company face every day. My promise to you is that I will handle this information with the greatest sensitivity, and will work to find the best solutions and outcomes for our future together.

You can choose to complete this survey anonymously or by name. Use as much space as you need. Feel free to attach additional pages.

Please complete and return no later than [date] at 12 p.m. Thank you in advance. I value your participation.

1. How can the company improve?

2. What are the area(s) in which you would like to improve and how can the company support you in achieving those goals?

3. How do your goals support the company?

4. What do you see as challenges within the company?

5. What do you see as possible solutions to those challenges?

6. Have you communicated concerns in the past? If so, were those concerns addressed?

7. Is your job description at [Our Company] clearly defined?

8. What do you most like about your position at [Our Company]?

9. What would you like your future to be at [Our Company]?

10. What's great about [Our Company]?

11. Do you have any additional comments or suggestions you would like to share?

When the surveys come back to you, look for the themes that run through responses. (It can help to go through them with an outsider like a coach, who may be able to spot patterns that you miss.) You may notice that everyone mentions problems with computer systems, or that communications issues come up. People may tell you over and over that they've raised concerns to you or their supervisors, and never seen anything change. The patterns you see will reveal the behavior and culture of the business—and they may be far different from what you believed you had created.

It can be unsettling, even infuriating, to discover you're still dealing with breakdowns and conflicts that you thought had been resolved long ago, or that seem easily avoidable. But focus on the value of what you now know. You may have been unaware of the problems surfacing in the survey, but you've been living with the effects of them every day. Now you have a choice about whether you want to address them and how.

One thing you'll probably notice is, while you may expect an outpouring of complaints about money and think that people will use this opportunity to lobby for better compensation, that usually doesn't happen. What I see most often are comments about people's interactions and connections in an office, or complaints about how they feel disconnected and unheard. People hunger to know that someone hears their truth, and because they may not have been asked for their input recently—or ever—you'll find that most of the answers have to do with the state of the company, and people's sense of their place in it.

This wealth of information from all levels of the business, added to your own observations, will sharply focus your perceptions of what's happening, what's not happening, and what you'd like to do next. You may discover that the biggest issues are, say, a breakdown in communication, or people working without job descriptions that define their responsibilities clearly. Survey comments may tell you that employees aren't sure they're doing the right thing, or that they were hired to do one kind of work, but have been diverted into a scramble of other projects. Or perhaps you prided yourself on doing away with meetings, but notice that people are complaining about having no way to check in with their larger work group or see the big picture of the business. You may find out that you're not giving people the clarity and direction they need from a leader.

What do you want to do about those issues?

That's the question that will take you to something new. Going deeper, the questions that will guide your strategy should be:

- What are these problems costing the business?

- If I correct them, what will the likely result be?

- What will I need to accomplish that?

This is the blueprint for an action plan that will let you focus on issues one by one, with clarity about why they're important. To solve a communication problem, you might ask a skilled communicator on the staff to offer lunchtime coaching, or bring in an HR person to make a presentation. You might institute meetings. To clear up confusion about responsibilities, maybe you'll set a timeline for reviewing everyone's responsibilities and updating job descriptions.

You'll be solving your most significant problems, motivated by a clear understanding of how they're connected to your business's larger purpose.

But before you switch into action mode, take one more giant step toward connection with your colleagues and employees by going over their feedback, human to human.

Conversations that feed connection

In many people's ideal world, it would be possible to go through the whole process I've just described without having a single in-person conversation. A lot of owners and managers feel as though they don't know what to say, or that it's easier and cleaner to handle things via e-mail or text, and skip the unpredictable back and forth.

But I encourage you to strengthen your relationship with the people in your business by scheduling follow-up conversations about the employee survey. Because I know you may feel unsure of what to say—or fall back on ways of communicating that will block the kind of connection you want, I'll walk you through some dos and don'ts and give you some sample scripts to get you started. You've done plenty of challenging things in your business. Give this a try. It can give you a powerful new way of connecting.

Make it safe, then question, listen, and suggest

You may be accustomed to walking into meetings focused on what you want to say and how you'll get the result you've decided you want. But if you do that when it's time to talk about the survey, you're likely to miss the opportunities that will come from connecting slowly, and listening to what comes up when you don't dominate the conversation.

I've mentioned safety before and I'll underline it here. Your first order of business is to establish a safe environment for communication. I don't mean to suggest that your office is a hazardous place. I'm talking about creating an environment—both for the purposes of this meeting and going forward in your business—in which people aren't on guard and defensive, expecting their ideas and feelings to be put down, ridiculed, dismissed, or attacked.

You can get practice creating safety in your survey meetings by handling them this way:

- Ask yourself: What's the best way to connect with this person and put him or her at ease? Then ask the individual directly: "I'd like to talk about your survey answers with you. Where would you be most comfortable doing that?" Give people a choice. It may feel safer to meet in a conference room in view of other people than to do it in your office. Let the other person decide.

- It's standard policy in most places today always to have another woman in the room if you are a male superior meeting with a female employee. That reinforces the feeling of safety as well. It's good policy to have another person as a witness to any conversation about personnel issues or discussions about how employees feel about their jobs and workplace. The idea is to choose a third party who is not threatening or on your side—you don't want to double-team the other person, you want to offer him or her support. The witness will not take notes, or speak. He or she will just listen.

- Explain that the meeting is private, and that everything said will remain confidential. *Honor that promise.*

- Explain the purpose of the meeting. "I wanted to meet with you today to talk about your survey responses. The purpose of doing that is to make your experience of working here better, and to make the business run better. I'm here to ask a few questions, but mostly to listen."

— Explain the structure of the meeting, and outline what you want to know. "We have about thirty minutes to talk, and in that time I'd like to know what you think is working here, what's not, and if you have any suggestions for me. I have your survey here, and if it's all right with you, we can use it as our guide. I'm mostly going to listen. If there's anything I need to share with you I will, but mostly I want to know what you think."

Structuring the meeting is not about control. It's another way of creating a feeling of safety. The other person knows what to expect, and doesn't have to worry about surprises.

Remember that conversations have to be led. It's not productive to open up a free-for-all in which someone takes an hour and a half to pour a decade's worth of problems on the table.

LOOK FOR OPPORTUNITIES TO CREATE OPENINGS and invite the other person to enter their own space. By that I mean ask questions then get out of the way and listen, without defensiveness, to what's true for them. Let *them* take the stage. To build trust and rapport, you must listen, and even if you disagree with their conclusions, validate their truth by acknowledging it. "I understand that you've been very frustrated by the way we do X. That's the way it was, and this is where we want to go. What do you think we can do to make things right?"

SET ASIDE JUDGMENT AND PROJECTION. If you enter the discussion with judgments about the other person, he or she will undoubtedly shut down or go instantly into a defensive mode. Once that happens, good communication has little chance to exist. But if you set aside judgment in favor of simply listening, you'll be amazed at what you can accomplish. It's a simple formula, really. Judgment is fear, and if you take the fear out of the equation, you'll get the best and most honest answers, the other person's greatest truth. That's how you'll find out what's been hidden from you, what you really need to know. It's also how you'll create a genuine connection.

DON'T GET STUCK. There's a difference between honoring people where they are and staying stuck in their stories. When someone tells me something like, "I've been putting up with this same crap for years, and this situation is never going to change," I say, "You could see it that way, or you could see that this process we're using today is providing more choice, and that's going to lead to different outcomes." In this process, you're always creating choice.

LOOK FOR THE "WHY." The stories people use to explain what's happening and how situations evolved are important, even if they're not true. They explain why people act the way they do, and why particular games are being played the way they are. *The opportunity for change is hidden in the why.*

Some of my clients say they don't want to know the "why" of a situation, and *there's a new school of transformational leadership theory that argues that since all of our stories are made up, none of them are true, and therefore they're not important.* But I completely disagree. Even if a story isn't true, it shapes our perceptions and reactions, and we have to deal with those perceptions to find a resolution. We either have to change the story or address it, because it shapes everything. You need to know the stories people are telling themselves about their work situation.

If someone is performing badly, you may think he or she is lazy or deficient. But the "why" will tell you what the situation looks like through the eyes of the bad performer, giving you at least some of the clues you need to see what's really happening. If the person's story is that she can't sell your product because the economy is bad—even though the rest of your staff's sales are through the roof, you can help defuse the story by listening, and adding perspective. If the story is that a staffer doesn't have proper training and support, or that a salesman doesn't like sales, you can move toward a solution that addresses that. When you know why, you can address the deep cause of problems.

DON'T RUSH IN TO CORRECT THE OTHER PERSON OR DEFEND YOUR POSITION. Instead, get curious about the way he or she sees things. Ask questions. It often happens that people simply want to vent, or resolve a problem by talking it through. If I notice that happening, I might say, "Okay, it sounds like you've just figured out what to do," and they realize they have.

When someone describes a problem to you, ask: "Do you have any ideas for making it better?" And if they seem stuck, offer suggestions, then ask: "What do you think?" Invite them into the conversation repeatedly, just as you would with a top client. Keep creating openings. Remember: You know how to do this. This is what you do to stay connected to clients. If you treat your employees with the same sensitivity you use with your clients, you'll never have a problem.

STAY OPEN, AND KEEP LISTENING. Some of the best solutions to your most difficult problems can come from what you learn in these conversations.

As you set aside judgment to listen and ask questions, you help people get authentic about what their truth is, which frees them to accept it. They may come in complaining about a bad boss and walk away realizing that they spend 70 percent of their workday doing something they hate, and boss or no boss, they won't be content until they change the focus of their job. Everyone you take through this process will get a sense of how they're both part of the problem and part of the solution, and you'll be able to design solutions built on people's strengths. When there's a bad fit, you'll realize it.

You'll get a good sense of who's well matched with their responsibilities, who's checked out, and who is the best fit for your team going forward. You'll also hear clearly where you're falling short, and what you need to change.

When you go back to your lists of problems and potential solutions, you'll have the voices and wisdom of your employees in your ear and know what pieces of the puzzle they can help you snap into place. Make it your priority to match people with their real passions, and to honor your "Not To Do" list so you can keep your own passions fired up. And keep talking. I recommend an employee review every six months. That may seem excessive, but if an employee is under-producing, do you really want to wait a whole year to address the issue? And if someone is full of ideas and energy, why not reward them more often—and strengthen their connection to you and the business?

Armed with the information you've gathered in the survey and your own reflection, you're no longer trying to fix the business in your imagination, the one running on your assumptions about how things are. You're dealing with the truth. You're in a position now to ensure that your business has integrity in every sense. In the next short chapter, I'll show you how to go forward, and how to avoid some of the most common hurdles that get in the way. I'll leave it to you to build your plan—you know how to set goals, and if you're not comfortable creating an action plan that breaks down what needs to be done into manageable steps with targets and accountability attached, you may want to work with a coach. What we'll focus on briefly in the next chapter is making sure that on the people level, you're leading effectively, and know how to defuse and rewire situations that undermine strong connection.

CHAPTER 5

Handling People Problems with Connected Communication

We've been fairly systematic so far in sizing up integrity and connection in the workplace. In this chapter, I want to set aside checklists and grids and coach you through some of the human problems—both other people's and yours—that are likely to come up as you carry out your business vision. The tools and advice you'll find here will take you from the potential overload of seeing the 3D reality of your business to explaining your plan and getting the best from the people on your team.

The mantra I've been repeating throughout the book holds true here: Change, authenticity, and success grow from the inside out. So keep touching base with yourself to be sure that before you turn the key on your plans, you feel genuinely connected to them. *Then* put the pedal to the metal.

This chapter speaks directly to the resistance, doubts, and confusion that inevitably come up as you stretch into new territory and take the risk of bringing passion and connection into what you do every day. Read it to get an overview of how to handle some of the most common scenarios you're likely to face, and keep it as a resource you can refer to when you hit a rough patch. Feel free to skim through the topics in this chapter to see what applies to you, but if you have any perfectionist tendencies, do not skip the material on perfectionism. And if you happen to work with either men or women, be sure to read the final section.

OVERWHELMED? REMEMBER: YOU KNOW WHAT TO DO. THIS IS YOUR SHOW.

When you haul a boat out of the water and take a walk around it, damage that's usually hidden below the water line glares back at you. So much so that it can be difficult to see anything but the cracks, chips, rust spots, and barnacles. Even if much of the equipment and structure is gleaming, it's easy to think you've got a wreck on your hands.

The same feeling can overwhelm you at the end of an integrity check and employee survey of your business or business life. The problems you hadn't seen can become the *only* thing you see—and that can be paralyzing.

One quick way to restore your confidence and optimism, if they've been challenged, is to look back at the history of your business. Let it play in your mind as though you're sitting in your living room, watching a sitcom on TV. This is your show. Pay attention to the good parts—the places where everything was going well and everyone was having a great experience. Who were the actors? What was happening? Why did it feel good to you? Why did it work so well?

Your mind might go straight to a particular highlight—the year when everything seemed to be clicking. That stretch when you couldn't wait to get to the office, because you were having so much fun, and feeling so satisfied, even when you were putting in sixty-hour weeks. Sink into what it felt like then.

You were enthusiastic, confident, even inspired. You liked what you were doing.

Who were you letting yourself be then? An intrepid adventurer instead of a fretting bean counter? An artist as well as an engineer? The best, most inspiring team leader you've ever been? You can call on that part of yourself, that identity, that role. Try it on again. See how it feels.

STUDY YOUR BUSINESS TIMELINE
TO CONNECT WITH WHAT WORKED

Now move through the "seasons" of the business. Season One: startup. Season Two: moving into a bigger office. And so on. What were your milestones? You got a big contract. Hired your first assistant. Joined forces with someone who was a perfect fit. Had a windfall project that gave you the confidence to expand, or try something new.

What pushed you to the next step? What turned things around, or opened doors for you? There's always a reason, a spark. Did a particular challenge light a rocket under you? Did you have a combination of people in place who created an unstoppable team? Did a particular supplier send you important business? Did you offer a program that customers loved? What made your successes come together? Have you got those elements in place today?

You've just finished sizing up some of the major assets of your business—the people. How do they compare with the ones in place when the business was at its best?

When someone tells me that a person who was a key catalyst in an office is gone now, we analyze why. Then we create a profile of the kind of person who works best in that position, a blueprint for what's needed. An office manager who was also a paralegal might've been the "special sauce" that helped law partners stay at the top of their game. Maybe a patient, outgoing front-office person kept everyone, including clients, energized and happy.

When you figure out what made the biggest difference, you can find it again.

ARE YOU STILL THE SAME PERSON, WITH THE SAME GOALS?

As you move forward on your timeline, notice the stress points as well. If your pleasure, profits, or sense of confidence have declined, look for what tipped things in that direction.

"Things were good until 2001," a client might tell me. "I had a lot of success. But then things started to erode." As we look at why, we might see that he hired someone who wasn't good for the business, or started to get away from his core work.

The factors may have nothing to do with the business itself. I often hear reasons like these:

- I got married/got into a relationship/wanted to help raise our new baby and I put less energy into the business.

- I got into a bad relationship, and it sucked my energy so I had less to put in at the office.

- Business started to get shaky and I lost all my good people because I couldn't afford to keep them.

- I've been in this business for a very long time and I'm ready for something new.

There are a million possibilities, and it's worth sifting through them to get an idea of which factors are still in place and what these turning points can teach you.

Where are you now? Do you still want what you used to want? When the baby grew up or the bad relationship ended, you may have assumed that you wanted to climb back to the helm of your business, throw yourself into it, and go for maximum growth or chase another expansive goal.

But do you? I've worked with many lawyers who are adamant about expanding—until they face the reality of larger staffs, astronomical overhead, and intensified pressure to produce. For those who realize smaller is better for them, new choices open up: partnering with someone, taking on an associate, refocusing with a new specialty. They're free of outgrown dreams.

CLARITY COMES FIRST:
WHAT'S IN THIS FOR YOU?

Plug into the feeling of being at your best, having fun, being excited by your work and colleagues. Will the goals you have in mind now let you have that feeling?

As your plans take shape and you prepare to set them in motion, what's your motivation for going the direction you have in mind? What are you getting out of it? (Money alone isn't enough.) Why do you want to reach the goals you've set? Can you be the person you most want to be at the center of this vision?

As I hope you've seen by now, authentic communication with yourself is 95 percent of the game. If you're feeling unclear, take the time to connect with your authentic self, and don't press on with a plan until you're clear about what you really want.

The Grid in chapter 3 can give you invaluable help. Use it to connect with the parts of yourself that you're using to make your decisions, and to be sure that you're including all the parts you value. Go back, with your new vision in mind, and run it through the questions on the Grid that attract you. Going forward, what do you want to see around you? What do you want to hear? How do you want to feel?

Build your plan around the information you've gathered, but keep your carefully honed vision at its core.

If you want additional support for your authentic self, flip back to the exercises at the end of chapter 1. A coach can be a great resource as well if you need a neutral sounding board.

You're ready to move forward when you can tell people what you want and take the proactive stance: "This is my choice. This is how we'll meet our challenges. This is what I want from you. This is what we're going to do."

It's a completely different experience from "We're going to take what comes, roll with it, and react." It's also different from "I'm just doing what I have to do."

In steering ahead by making deliberate choices, rather than simply reacting, you're stepping into your truth, playing a bigger game.

COMMIT. PERIOD.

You know that integrity is the cement that binds all the elements of your business. When you announce a plan, your personal integrity must be impeccable. Never launch something you can't follow through on. What you communicate to everyone around you when you make a plan and change it the next day or week is that the plan doesn't matter, the changes you're asking them to make don't matter, and they don't matter. If you are not 100 percent committed to follow-through, don't bother starting.

Commitment means that even if you have a couple of bad months after you institute the plan, you stay the course instead of freaking out. You're making the shift to a proactive reality instead of a reactive one. You're working toward a particular vision, on your chosen course, rather than steering around potholes and losing your sense of direction.

You're not running a MASH unit. You don't have to react dramatically to every upset, crisis, or unforeseen development. You can stick to your plan if you prepare for both bumps in the road and wind at your back.

MANY PLANS ARE ABANDONED BECAUSE OF FEAR. Leaders who don't want to lead don't trust themselves, and go back on their word. They doubt, doublespeak, and fall back into reactive patterns.

Doubt and fear are normal, but they don't have to run your business. Take time to work out for yourself what you want, rather than running to react. Say, "I'm going to take that under advisement. I'll get back to you tomorrow [or later in the week] with my decision."

MANY PLANS ARE DROPPED BECAUSE OF SUCCESS. Things can start moving fast, and as success builds, I'll often hear people say: "We got busy and forgot our procedures. I know what we're supposed to be doing, but we're just focused on cranking right now."

I get it that success can feel like a tornado carrying you to the Emerald City. But if that happens, step back, reassess, and remember your life is as important as the business. It may be that spending time with the family, exercising with a trainer, or meeting friends for dinner keeps you sane. Start asking: Whom can I hand things to? What procedures do I need to put in place to make that feel safe? What would it mean to add more staff? How can we clone what's working well?

A common scenario I see in working with small firms is that people start out doing what they're good at and become so successful that their business needs to expand. With more staff comes the need for systems and management, but typically, people who start out as lawyers and other professionals don't want to take on those tasks. So they avoid that aspect of the business. They let their employees manage themselves—and when there is no outside manager or accountability, things quickly turn chaotic.

When I suggest that they need to turn the management duties over to someone with the proper skill set, they often resist, saying, "I can't afford a manager," or "This is my firm, and I've got to be in charge of things."

But the truth is, they're never going to take on the job or do it right, even if it's essential, because they don't like doing it. It's not an authentic reflection of what they want, and pretending that things are otherwise will only compound the problem. I don't care if you're from the "grin and bear it" generation, where duty rules and choice is for wimps. That old "wisdom" will get you just so far. The world moves much faster than it used to, and the way people and technology function within it has changed drastically.

Evolution happens. Change is unstoppable. Through it all, commit to your vision. And commit to keeping that vision authentic, connected to who you are—and *the person you will become* as you grow.

COMMUNICATE AND LEAD

When you know what you want in your business, your job is to lead, to explain to people, "This is where we're going, and this is how we're getting there."

Keep the lines of communication open, and be clear about the changes you are going to make. You will need to tell each employee exactly what you expect from them, how you expect them to be accountable for their responsibilities, and what they can expect from you. It's hard, but if you expect integrity, you have to deliver it, too.

Some of what you'll be doing is patching holes in your infrastructure. If you found that there are integrity problems involving the way people use time, for example, you may institute a set workday for the first time, telling people, "I expect you to be at your desk working from nine a.m. until five p.m.," or set guidelines for using time more effectively by deciding, "I'd like to make our meetings more focused by having us turn off our phones."

You may assign someone to develop new protocols for dealing with clients, or handling paperwork. You may set up communication training.

Whatever the particulars, you will be bringing change into your environment, and some people won't like it. Ask people for their honest opinions, acknowledge their fears, and make adjustments if you need to. Once you put your changes in motion, hold people accountable for following the rules. Be sure to track everything that you implement, as it creates buy-in and measurable progress. That's the part of integrity having to do with a unified team of people rowing in the same direction.

People pull hard for each other if you give them a chance. I worked with a business that had hit a significant slowdown, and the owners realized that to meet payroll until things turned around, they'd either need to lay off a significant slice of the staff or ask everyone to take cuts in pay. I suggested that they pair the pay-cut option with an incentive program, offering bonuses to those who exceeded their revenue goals each month. When the owners posed the options—layoffs vs. pay cut with incentives—to the staff, the employees overwhelmingly supported the pay-cut plan. And in the first month, everyone exceeded their targets and collected bonuses, not only keeping their income intact but driving it up as they lifted the business.

Some common people problems

This isn't a management text, but I want to point out a few difficult-people scenarios that can arise as you are putting your plan in place. Remember that you're always looking to shore up authenticity by acting with integrity yourself—doing what you said you'd do—and by encouraging people to do the jobs that are the most satisfying to them. Sometimes those jobs will be within your business, and sometimes, they'll be elsewhere.

SABOTAGE. A single change-resistant person can take a company down. In one business I worked with, a longtime office manager resisted the recovery plan the owners were trying to put in place. He undermined their authority with his complaints to clients and colleagues and in his direct reports. It's important to confront such people with their behavior and its effects, listen to their explanation, and explain what will happen if the behavior doesn't change. I was direct with the office manager, telling him, "What you're doing could tank this firm." I listened to his explanations and rationalizations, most of which had to do with fear-based problems or control issues. Be open to the other person's responses, and open to the possibility that they'll want to learn and change. But if that isn't happening, stick to your HR protocols and follow through as you said you would. When you know a person needs to go, let him or her go.

MAKING A DIFFICULT CHANGE. As you compare your current operation with your vision of a connected workplace—all of you in jobs you're well suited to, supporting each other and thriving—you'll find instances where a current employee is a bad match for your future. It's quite possible that in your business until now, enthusiasm and commitment to excellence haven't been a requirement. (I've seen standards as low as "cheap bodies filling seats.") It's even more likely that you've been avoiding the tough conversation you'd have to have if you wanted to replace a problem staffer.

Here's one way to communicate with an employee when you want to clarify and end a situation that can't continue. I advocate

117

being clear, direct, and kind—and always following the protocols your HR department has in place:

"Jim, I know you've been in charge of ABC for us, but that's no longer working. It can no longer happen. Do you understand?

"We need to make a change because keeping you in that position is causing XYZ. Do you understand?"

Sometimes, you'll have another option for the person: training to offer, a position that's a better fit, or a compassionate exit package. When someone clearly needs to go, a severance package of several months' salary can be a liberating option that allows you to make a change while defusing the employee's survival fears and allowing him or her to stay open to new choices.

HIRING REALISTICALLY, AND WELL. When you've taken the time to think about exactly what you want in the person who will play an important role in your business (*every* person should fit that description), it's vital to take your needs seriously enough to communicate them clearly to potential hires—especially when those requirements go beyond the typical job description.

I once helped a law firm hire a new attorney, and some candidates seemed surprised when asked, "How do you feel about teaching?" I explained that the firm had a young paralegal who'd need training, and the lawyer to be hired would be in charge of training her and imparting knowledge about the firm's needs and flow of cases. More than one person told me straightaway, "I love the law, and I love this business, but I'm a terrible teacher." I turned away a number of excellent candidates who said the same thing—because while teaching had nothing to do with being a lawyer, it was central to what was needed from the person in that position. (The firm eventually hired an ambitious attorney who told me, "I love to teach!" and talked enthusiastically about the mentoring she'd done.)

ACKNOWLEDGING AND FIXING HIRING MISTAKES. Occasionally, you'll be authentic in describing what you need, but the other person will be less than authentic in talking about their willingness to do what needs to be done, and you'll find you've hired badly. That happened at another law firm I worked with, when we brought on a smart young lawyer to take a position that would probably have been done by someone with much less training at another firm. We warned her it was work typically given to paralegals.

The young lawyer had stars in her eyes, and saw the job as a chance to be mentored by the head of the prestigious firm so she could climb into his highly specialized field. He, in turn, saw her as someone he could probably show the ropes of the business—if she were willing to start at the bottom and put in a good number of hours doing unglamorous, nuts-and-bolts work first.

It was a bad match. Files piled up on the young lawyer's desk, wreaking havoc with the work flow in the office, and she couldn't shake her resentment at not being able to do the more sophisticated work she had been trained for. She was disappointed, bitter, and developing physical symptoms—migraines, stomach trouble—when I met her. The boss was disappointed as well. He'd been sincere. He wanted to work closely with her. But for the next year or two or three, he needed someone devoted to doing the work at hand, someone willing to master it from the ground up. "I see a great future for her, but she needs to grow," he said. "What she's shown me is that she can't take direction, and she's not respectful. I can't put her in front of one of our big clients. She needs grounding to handle that kind of interaction, and she's not ready for that. I can't give her what she wants right now, and she doesn't want to work up to it."

The young lawyer cried when we called her in to talk about the work she'd been neglecting, but she also seemed relieved. As you help people get authentic about what's true for them in a situation, it frees them. They can see how they may be a part of the problem, and they finally understand the real reasons why they're unhappy or struggling.

Accepting that she hated what she was doing, with the physical complaints to prove it, she decided to move to a new law firm, where she could use the skills she had worked so hard to acquire. She's thriving now. And so is the office she left behind, where a contented paralegal is beautifully executing the work the lawyer hated, and doing it with pride.

It can be wrenching to fire someone, but keeping someone secure in a job they can't take pride in or do well does them no favors. It's unrealistic to expect that every person on your team will be doing the work that's his or her life's passion. (Some people may be working to help support that passion—think of all those waiters whose strongest desire is to act.) But it's reasonable and necessary to expect that each person you hire will be devoted to doing excellent work as they carry out the responsibilities you assign, and that they'll *want* to fit in. If they won't or can't, you'll damage your integrity, as well as that of your business and the employee, if you don't help them move on.

GET A GRIP ON
YOUR OWN PERFECTIONISM

High standards are good. Impossible-to-reach standards are frustrating, demoralizing, and sometimes paralyzing.

Many businesses are started and run by people who believe that only perfection is good enough, and demand that they, and anyone who works for them, aim for that elusive, unattainable ideal. Perfectionism can turn a three-hour project into a fifteen-hour ordeal, or label a perfectly good report a "disaster." It's delayed many a product launch and sales campaign, and it's squeezed the life out of more staffs than I can count.

The drive for perfection is an occupational hazard among lawyers, whose documents must be accurate, and whose training has drilled into them that mistakes are unacceptable. But it's possible to be accurate without crossing the line into "it's perfect or it's nothing," an attitude that's poison wherever you find it. In the auto industry, in real estate and every kind of service and sales, I've run into members of the ultra-critical tribe. They walk in cloaked in judgment and tear into everything they touch with so much ferocious energy that nothing will ever be good enough for them.

As I tell my clients often, there's an important distinction to make between perfectionism and excellence. The roots of the word excel are "beyond" and "lofty." Excellence requires reaching, and reaching can be risky. You can be brilliant, surpass your limits—and fall. Becoming excellent often involves learning from mistakes that turn out to be springboards to the next breakthrough.

But perfect, as used by perfectionists, means "flawless." Perfectionism, as I've seen it practiced, is about being bulletproof, armored even, with a heavy dose of cover-your-ass and a real aversion to human vulnerability. Can you feel the difference between the energy of reaching for excellence and the clenched fear of "What if it's not perfect?" There ain't a lot of joy in a perfectionist, and there's even less appreciation or praise. Instead, there's a relentless desire to root out even the tiniest flaw—because anything flawed is worthless. But what does that say about the value of humans who are, by nature, full of flaws? I'm no psychologist, but I've noticed that perfectionism seems closely related to the kind of self-criticism that says, "I'm not good enough—so I need to go to extreme lengths to prove I'm at least all right."

Perfectionists can get mired in micro concerns, and lose sight of the big picture. I joke with my perfectionist clients that if Jesus himself handed them the New Testament, they'd get out the red pen and start marking it up. They don't know when or how to stop being critical of everything. One attorney I worked with was reviewing papers with an associate for a client, and stopped at a particular document with a scowl on his face. "What idiot wrote this piece of crap?" he said. "I can't believe anyone let this go out."

The associate smiled. "The idiot who wrote it? That was you. Six months ago."

If you're a perfectionist, you're in a bind. You probably think you can't trust anyone but yourself with the details. And it's that kind of thinking that keeps a $475-per-hour attorney doing clerical work that a $20-per-hour admin person could easily handle.

If you see yourself in that mirror, I'd like to ask you: Do you value your knowledge?

If you did, you couldn't hold your staff to the same standard you hold yourself. Proper training of staff and imparting experts' knowledge to them can solve the error problem in 99 percent of the law firms I have worked with. But the problem isn't really errors. It's the perfectionists' judgmental thought process, which feeds their fear—and robs them of opportunity and the ability to move forward.

Coaching can help you come to terms with the fear. So can counseling, which has gotten great results for many of my clients. When you change the way you see the world, and yourself, opportunities expand.

IF YOUR PERFECTIONISM
ISN'T LEAVING ANYTIME SOON...

For the sake of argument, let's say you know you're a perfectionist, and you don't have any immediate plans to try to change that. What then?

You can make life a thousand times easier for those you work with by acknowledging to yourself and to your staff that they will never be able to make you happy. I've frequently been asked to help people have this conversation with their staff, and it has moved offices many notches up the happiness scale.

In one company, a female staff member broke down in tears when her perfectionist boss, who is a father figure to her, criticized her work harshly. As the three of us talked about the problem, we came to this: The woman was caught up in trying to make her boss happy, not getting the job done. Not only was the effort failing, she was falling behind in her work as she tried to perfect every atom of it before turning it in.

"It doesn't matter what you do," I told her. "He's not going to be happy." The boss nodded. "This is a game that can't be won. His perfectionism isn't about your work, it's about him. It's who he is—he wants to tweak and change everything. That's about him. If he loses his temper, that's about him too. It's not about you."

Simply knowing that allowed the woman to focus on her job again, the do-able part she was capable of handling easily. A truth was established for her: "This is not about me. I don't have to manage his shit. I'm not a little girl who has to please Daddy. This is what is. I am here to do the work, and I choose to stay and do it well."

Both she and the boss, facing the situation honestly, were able to go forward. She realized that criticism from him was not about her not being good enough, and it wasn't about her losing her job. It was about the way her perfectionist boss processed work. The boss, for his part, was finally able to apologize for his outbursts, and let her know he recognized the value she was delivering.

For some people, staying with a perfectionist boss will only be crazy-making. For some, though, putting an end to the unwinnable "try to please the perfectionist" game makes it possible to restore confidence and connection.

THE RULE OF THE POWER OF DISTINCTION: YOU CONTROL THE MEANING OF YOUR EXPERIENCES

Years ago, in a training program, I was introduced to a concept that I've used repeatedly over the years to shift people's responses to what they're experiencing and strengthen their connection to what serves them. The idea, called "The Rule of the Power of Distinction," says you can make anything mean what you want it to mean. You assign meaning to any given situation or circumstance.

- You get fired. Is that a tragedy you'll never recover from or a gift that liberates you to do something that has meaning for you? You get to decide.

- Business is bad. Does that mean you've lost your touch? That no one can thrive in the lousy economy? That it's time to pack up? That you need to go back and do some integrity checks on your operation? You get to decide.

- People are resisting part of your new plan. Is that evidence that they "just don't get it" and need to be replaced? Is it a reason to chuck the whole thing, because if you can't sell this, nothing will change? Or does it mean you need to go back and review what you've communicated? You get to decide.

Some interpretations of events will set you spiraling into self-recrimination, blame, resignation, or hopelessness. (Frankly, those aren't your best looks.) Other interpretations will feed your resilience. Which do you prefer?

One of my clients watched with dismay as it became clear that the next U.S. president was going to be someone he didn't trust or support. "You know what that means?" he told me. "If that bozo gets in, my business will be shit for the next four years. The economy will be crap. We'll get regulations coming at us from all sides. It's going to be a disaster."

"Well, if you're really wedded to that idea, I guess I should just get my things and leave now," I told him. "If you believe that's what's going to happen, that will happen for you. There are millions of other Americans with a different idea of what this will mean, and their experience will probably be better than yours.

"I don't care about your politics," I told him. "But if you are firm in thinking that your business is going to be down the toilet for the next four years, it's going to go down."

Do your attitudes have that much power? Yes, they do. *What you expect you get*—so upgrade your expectations.

The good news is that my client decided that no matter who was president, he could run his business in the smartest, most connected way possible. He had a chain of record years during that same president's administration. What does he want to make that mean? That everything he's known about politics and business his whole life is wrong? Or maybe that he's got the chops to thrive no matter who's in office?

You can change your sense of connection to a situation in a minute by choosing to interpret it in a way that gives you the power to choose positive actions instead of a victim mentality.

HELPING PEOPLE MAKE BETTER DISTINCTIONS

As you're explaining a plan to the people you're working with, you can address their fears directly by using the power of distinction to explain what you mean: "X means this. It doesn't mean that." For instance, "This new schedule doesn't mean I think anyone is slacking off. It means that I want to give us all more accountability, because we work better that way."

The more you do this, the more people can learn to stop and look at their automatic expectations and conclusions so they can shift them if they don't like what they see.

Given how slippery meaning can get when we're all imposing our own interpretations, I also strongly suggest defining terms every time you set a goal or have an important conversation. When I'm working with businesspeople who tell me, "Things have got to change around here," I'm careful to find out what they mean. What specific things? And what precisely does change mean? What does that look like to them? Don't assume that you and the rest of the world are speaking the same language. Keep clarifying.

In the workplace,
we are men and women first

One of the most confusing parts of dealing with people in the workplace is navigating the differences between men and women. I know I'm in touchy territory here, even bringing up the subject, because in modern business, we're supposed to ignore gender differences and treat everyone without bias. We assume that means "treat everyone as if we're all the same." The problem is, we're not all the same. Instead, each person is navigating between the pulls of their masculine and feminine sides, and trying to relate to the masculine and feminine in each other. I'm not saying we're all nothing but cavemen and cavewomen under our business attire, but primal instinct runs us more than we admit, and understanding it can make a huge difference in how well we get along and get our business done.

I've been heavily influenced in my thinking by people like author David Deida, who describes the masculine and feminine in ways that I find both useful and true, and by Alison A. Armstrong, who looks at these gender differences from a complementary perspective through a woman's eyes.

The next chapter, on connecting in personal relationships, will go into this topic in much greater depth, but because it's so important—and ignored—in the business world, I wanted to mention it here, as we consider the people issues that can arise in your teams.

Since World War II, women have streamed into the workplace, and in some job categories, they make up more than half of the workforce. They've risen to executive positions and taken on some of the most demanding jobs out there, and as they've done so, they've been required to embrace more masculine values of competition, focus, and achievement. That's sometimes led them to set aside more feminine values of connection, appreciation, and free-flowing creativity.

(To repeat: I'm not saying that all men are competitive and all women want connection. I'm saying that the masculine and feminine parts of ourselves value these things, and again, all of us contain both masculine and feminine. It's when these energies get out of balance within individuals and between people that trouble occurs.)

As women embrace the masculine, sometimes the men they work with respond with more feminine energy, and that can bring confusion and conflict that no one understands until they address the problems on a man-woman level.

I'd like to give you one vivid example:

The partners in a business called me in because they believed that one of the women in the firm was out of control and bringing down the business. Though Theresa was one of the highest producers in the firm, she was perpetually angry, screaming at the staff and dominating meetings with rants and demands. Her male peers stepped back and acquiesced because they didn't know what else to do. She knew they all depended on the revenue she brought in, and she could do whatever she wanted. But her decisions were not always the best for the firm as a whole and it was demoralizing the place. What could they do?

I saw Theresa in action in a meeting, and then spent time with both sides. Any time I see behavior as aggressive as this woman's, I look for where there's fear and insecurity, because that kind of anger is almost always a mask worn by someone feeling unsafe. Theresa was a striver who had graduated at the top of her law school class and come up through a high-pressure firm where she competed with the best.

"That's an impressive background," I told her. "You've been ambitious, you've accomplished all this—it's awesome. But whether you're a man or woman, if you strive to be the best, there's always a price to pay. In an environment like this, I believe the emotional price for women is much higher simply because much of the work they do is very masculine in nature— high-pressure, highly detail-oriented work that's full of deadlines and pressure to produce. I'm not talking about ability or brains, I'm talking about our basic natures. Think about the true essence of the feminine. The feminine is fluid—it changes directions in an instant, and then changes again for what seems like no reason. That's part of the magic or imagination of a little girl. It's not linear and goal-driven. That's not to say women can't function well in a linear, goal-driven environment. Plenty of women do. But when they decide to do that, I think it is essential for them to nurture that feminine side of themselves, whatever that means to them."

Theresa knew why I was there, so I asked her why she thought there was conflict in the firm. She let me know that she was suffering and frustrated, but not clear about why. When I asked how she managed the pressures in the firm, she started to cry.

"How do you take care of yourself?" I asked her.

She thought long and hard. She told me she had been neglecting her needs for years, not just in her professional life, but in her personal life as well. "How do I take care of myself?" she mused aloud. She wasn't sure.

When I asked her what she did for fun, she said that she loved to sing in the choir at her church, dance, get massages, and shop, and as she ran through that list, her energy shifted and lightened. But it fell again when she admitted she hadn't done any of that in a long time.

In a roundabout way, I suggested that she turn down the masculine impulse, which was always competing, and step away from its constant pressure. "Do the things that are going to nurture the little girl," I told her. "I'm not telling you how to be or what to do. But it's important to make a conscious effort to take care of the feminine part of you."

She said she'd book a massage that day.

I had just one message for the men: "Man up." In the face of Theresa's emotional storms, they retreated, giving her what she wanted simply because they didn't want to deal with the anger. "The problem is that when you abandon a woman in a storm, it makes her worse, not better," I explained. "In a sense, her feminine side feels abandoned, and unprotected. Next time, you have to hold on until it passes. Where are your guts?"

"You don't understand," one of them said. "She's so difficult. And if we wait, it'll all blow over."

But I persuaded them to say no when they meant no, and to hold firm instead of caving.

As the gender roles balanced in the firm, the storming stopped. Theresa tended her neglected feminine side, and she began to relax some of her relentless striving. She was able to stop insisting that her way was the only way. The men, for their part, took back their integrity and began laying out their positions instead of automatically accepting hers. That seemed to empower them in their dealings with clients, and the revenue imbalance began to right itself as well.

I know it's tempting to say this gender stuff is a meaningless distraction. But I use it because it works. As long as Theresa stayed locked in her masculine side, and the men kept retreating, there was no good solution to the problem.

But when they accepted that they needed to work out the primal masculine/ feminine issues first, they could connect in a healthy way—and get on with the business of working together to serve clients and make money.

We'll look at more of the whys and hows of these basic man-woman relationships in the next chapter.

PART III

Connection in Dating, Marriage, Family, and Spiritual Life

N ow let's take a turn toward the personal. In this section, we'll leave the office behind to enter the realm of the heart and the spirit. One thing I've noticed is that much as we might try, none of us can segment our lives, walling off one part from another. Once you begin bringing your authentic self into any aspect of your life, it wants to push into the others. I often see my business clients start reaching for the tools of connection they've used in the office to help them at home.

I'm a passionate student of connection, and in the final chapters of the book I'd like to share what I've learned about how the skills of authenticity and openness can enhance the relationships that mean the most to us—the ones with friends, lovers, our children, even God—and teach you specific techniques for doing that. We often think of emotions as volatile energies that operate outside our control, but I hope you've noticed that this book is full of tools for stepping outside the frame and noticing the emotions and dynamics that come into play as you try to connect with yourself and others. When you stop to see them, you can choose the way you respond.

My deepest belief is that the way to change the world for the better is to express your authentic gifts, talents, and visions, and to build relationships of every kind that encourage other people to do the same. I think we can feed those relationships and ourselves by connecting with God, however we envision that great spirit, in the same genuine way.

These chapters will feel different from the ones you've seen so far—they're more personal, closer to the bone. They'll refine your understanding of connection, and let you experiment with going deeper to improve your dating life, your marriage, the life you have with your kids. When you bring self-understanding, openness, and compassion into those arenas, the potential for growth and for love is enormous.

You'll probably feel vulnerable, and a little naked, as you take the risk of going for the strong connections you've always wanted in this arena. I know I did. But let me assure you, it's the most rewarding thing I've ever done. If my experience and that of my friends and clients is any indication, it's likely to be the same for you.

I hope you'll let your authentic self lead, and explore the possibilities.

CHAPTER 6

Getting Real Connection in Dating and Mating

You meet someone new, answer a smile with a smile, start to talk. And if you're lucky, the more time you spend together, the more you realize how much there is to discover—and how much you want to. This person's company makes you feel so good. In the mirror of these new eyes, you realize there's more to you than you thought you could be, something this friend, then lover, sees, appreciates, and brings out in you. You expand each other, believe in each other, and both of you start to get the feeling that the longer you're together, the more there is to this new thing called "Us." It's huge. It's amazing. It fills you up.

Big fireworks go off inside when you realize that *this* is what you've got. It may happen as you begin to date, or after years of knowing someone, or even after a breakup, when suddenly both of you can see clearly what you had, and what you've lost.

I'm talking about the connection of big love, that pull toward another person that has the effect of opening you as you've never opened before. It can feel as if you've been packed all your life into a tight bud, never—till now—experiencing the beauty of unfolding and relaxing into all you could be with someone else. You're the real you, reveling in the real them. That's the love all of us want so much, the love so many of us struggle with finding and keeping.

Love's funny. The more we think we can outsmart it, the more it likes to show us who's boss. (Hint: It's not you if you think you've got a magic formula for taming it.) In the age of eHarmony, Match.com, OkCupid, and Tinder, we think we can sort through options with a quick thumbs up/thumbs down, identify exactly what we want as if we're ordering off a menu, and find the perfect partner. Sometimes it feels as though we've reduced the romance of love to a checklist.

The challenges grow as we work to keep the sparks arcing and the passion hot in long-term relationships. The going gets tricky, because once we're coupled up, it's easy to think we've mastered love. We believe we can use the same strategies that brought us together to keep that love "perfect."

But in dating and mating, love doesn't work that way. It evolves as we do, and the only way to flow with that, beginning to end, is to find ways to stay open to our partners—and to the possibility of deep connection—even when we want to close down because of rejection or fear or the sudden feeling of, "Oh my God. My spouse is a stranger."

This chapter is devoted to openness and the love it makes possible. In it, I'll show you the best ways I know to cultivate openness while looking for love and while tending to your partner and yourself in a relationship. I'll ask you to use your head as well as your heart. Some of what I'll be talking about may seem overly cerebral to you, but everything I'll show you is designed to help you experience what so many of us want more than anything—the deep soul connection of real, authentic love.

What are you open to?

DATING: IT'S A JUNGLE OUT THERE.
GUESS WHO'S PLAYING THE ANIMALS?

Feel that magnet drawing your eyes toward a good-looking guy or woman across the room? One of the most powerful human desires is to connect with a mate, and biology primes us to feel the pull of traits that signal good health and vitality—her shiny hair, wide hips, ample bottom, and breasts; his broad shoulders and strong build. In the most basic Tarzan terms, He = protector, She = mother/nurturer.

There's much, much more to us than that, of course. Our brains. Our full range of emotions. Our hearts and spirits. Most of us are fairly certain that modern relationships are about connecting the whole of us to another person. We've left the jungle, after all. This is the twenty-first century, where some women run countries and some men stay home to raise children.

But the truth is, for all our sophistication, deep down we *are* still wired like cavemen and cavewomen. Those primal circuits, and the expectations they create, can run—and often ruin—your love life if you're not conscious of how they work. But when you understand what triggers your primal circuitry, you can suddenly see the hidden dynamics at play both in yourself and in partners or potential partners. And you can learn to use those dynamics in new, conscious ways to build male-female friendships and love relationships that are deep, authentic, and satisfying.

A note on terminology: I'll be talking about men and women here, but as I mentioned in the previous chapter, I'm really talking about us as people who contain both masculine and feminine energies in different balances. It generally happens that males possess and express more of the masculine and women express more of the feminine. But the masculine/feminine balance runs along a continuum, and we need to understand both sides to thrive. What I say about men speaks to what's true for the masculine side of us, and what I say about women focuses on the feminine that we all possess.

In the modern world it is especially important that we understand the potential hidden dynamics and assumptions in our relationships, because the roles men and women fulfill in both relationships and the business world have changed dramatically. Younger couples are often living very different lives than their parents and grandparents did and facing new challenges. It doesn't matter if you're a couple coming from vastly different cultural or religious backgrounds, a dual-earner couple struggling to equitably split child-care duties, a stay-at-home dad and working mom negotiating territory that feels nothing like a '50s-era sitcom, a blended family raising stepchildren together, or any of a thousand variations on modern relationships. The tools and insights in this book can help you bring hidden assumptions and dynamics into the light and connect with one another authentically, allowing love to flourish and enabling you to face your challenges effectively together.

CAVEMAN/CAVEWOMAN, UPDATED

The most helpful guides I've found to the territory of masculine and feminine have been the authors I mentioned in the last chapter: David Deida, whose book *The Way of the Superior Man* is required reading for all my male clients, and Alison Armstrong, who helps men and women understand each other with books such as *Making Sense of Men: A Woman's Guide to a Lifetime of Love, Care and Attention from All Men.*

Both of them acknowledge that the "caveman" (my term, not theirs) goal for men and women in relationships is chemistry, that cocktail of sexual attraction our bodies cook up when someone sparks our attention. In dating, that's often the ultimate test—no chemistry, no next date.

But what do men *really* want? In *The Way of the Superior Man,* Deida explains that men's deepest motivation comes from "discovering their deepest truth, enjoying total freedom and love, and giving their fullest gifts." They're looking for women who will support and inspire them in the quest to find these.

Women, Armstrong suggests, want to carry their vision into the world, with men as their complements and partners (not saviors).

They want men who will spend time with them, take care of them, protect them, contribute to their well-being, and try to make them happy.

The frustration comes when chemical attraction doesn't get either side what it really wants for the long run—and I can tell you that there are a lot of men and women out there who managed to get what they thought they wanted (chemistry/sex) without ever figuring out how to find the connection they crave so badly.

The interesting point that comes up in both Deida and Armstrong is that authenticity is Love Potion #9. For women, the dating/partnering puzzle has always been "How do I find a nice guy who wants to know me and take care of me, not just get me into bed?" And for men, one perpetual quandary is "How do I find someone who will not only sleep with me, but will love me for who I am?" The answer in both cases comes back to: Be more of who you are, and love your mission and your interests passionately. Doing *that* will attract the partner you want.

This advice runs counter to much conventional wisdom and behavior. Guys and women both think they have to impress the object of their interest by puffing up their online dating profiles, hiding any perceived weaknesses, and saving their passion for, say, loud Hawaiian shirts, old comics, Aerosmith, and other such "uncool, low-rent" stuff for close friends who won't judge.

One popular tactic is to agree, agree, agree, while hiding your own "embarrassing" details. Introduced to a beautiful lawyer in a curve-hugging little black dress, it's easy for a guy who hates classical music to say, "Oh, you like Beethoven? Me too. Maybe we could go to a concert." A woman might nod, agree, and pump an appealing guy with questions about himself while withholding details about the animal rescue work that's her passion, because "I don't want him to think I'm a crazy cat lady."

Personally, I've been on both sides of the table. I know all too well how hard it is to be myself—flaws, quirks, opinions, and all—when I'm really attracted to a woman. When I've been with a woman I don't have deep feelings for, someone I don't care that much about impressing, it's been much easier to be real. And wouldn't you know it, those are the women who have often been strongly attracted to me.

Especially when the stakes are high—when we're powerfully drawn to the other person—it easy to try to let that chemistry do the talking, and shut out the authentic self. But chemistry has only one thing to say to a potential partner: I'll be whatever you want me to be so we can get to the main event—ripping each other's clothes off.

If chemistry's compromises get you past the preliminaries and into courtship or a relationship, you can wind up with a bit of a problem: a potential partner who's attracted to a "you" who isn't you at all.

These topics were on the table at a relationship workshop I led recently with my colleague Molly Lyda, a coach and marriage and family therapist whose primary focus is working with women. One of our aims was to help people understand the masculine/feminine balance inside themselves and in their relationships, and at one point we split the group in half, with Molly teaching the women, and me talking to the men.

The masculine essence is directive and single-focused, I told my group. It evolves and develops through curiosity, adventure, and exploring the unknown, even into recklessness. It thrives on the hunt and is greatly drawn to the challenge and the mystery of the feminine. Rigidity and purpose are primal survival instincts of the masculine, as it provides protection for the feminine *and to any children.*

Mission and adventure are paramount for the masculine, more important even than family, and the masculine is best expressed when men live their purpose and are fully present in their lives, rather than checked out. Only by moving through our greatest fears and trials do we come to a place of masculine wisdom and peace.

If your partner knows she can push you off your purpose, I told my group, she will see it and feel it as a sign of weakness. When men honor their masculine essence, they're in the strongest position to give the feminine what it seeks.

You can get a vivid image of the archetypal masculine if you think of early man, the hunter, whose survival depended on single-mindedly tracking and killing game so he and his family could eat. That's the essence we carry into the present.

With the young men at my workshop, I talked at length about the importance of understanding women's deep need for safety, and what a powerful undercurrent that is in male/female interactions. I recalled for them a striking moment from one of Armstrong's seminars: She asked the largely female crowd, "In the last six months, how many of you have been in fear for your life?" *Ninety-five percent* of the women raised their hands. Only three guys did—two were just back from Afghanistan, and the other was a cop.

Armstrong asked the women to give examples of what triggered their fear, and everyone who spoke had a story of walking back to her car in a parking structure, with a creepy guy not far behind her, or getting onto an elevator with a man who made her want to get off at the next floor, or passing a man on the street who whispered, or even yelled, a lewd comment about what he wanted to "do to her."

To understand women, I told my guys at the workshop, you have to understand that feeling of vulnerability and fear and how much they look to the masculine to help ease it. I'm not saying women are weak—in many ways they are much stronger than men are—but I am saying that they're much more concerned about safety than men tend to be.

We talked about how the masculine can comfort and delight the feminine by taking the lead in the relationship rather than falling into the pattern of "whatever you want, honey." The idea is not to be controlling or domineering, but to complement the feminine by offering a welcome channel for its free-flowing energy—and the sense of safety that comes from masculine decisiveness and direction.

Molly talked with the women about what the feminine looks like and needs, and how that essence speaks to the masculine. Her definition is fittingly poetic:

"The essence of the feminine," she says, "is fluid, sensitive, creative, nonlinear, introspective, nurturing, and thoughtful. She is the giver of life, including the birthing of babies, ideas, purpose, and passion. The feminine is curve and movement, breath and beauty. She is a circular, enfolding, powerful presence that affects everything in her realm and gives life to herself and others."

Where the masculine is single-focused, feminine consciousness spills in every direction, because every part of the environment is relevant to her and has clues for survival. Being generally smaller and weaker physically than men are, women evolved the ability to pay attention to everything, with a kind of diffuse awareness that today takes in everything from the socks on the floor to the child screaming down the hall. She may not be able to outrun or overpower trouble, but she's hardwired with the consciousness to anticipate it and move out of its way.

Another ancient feminine survival skill is adaptation, the ability to fit in with the tribe of the man who will ensure that a woman and her children will be taken care of. In modern life, Molly told her group, this ability to adapt can be an advantage, or it can play out as having a weaker sense of self and going with the flow—even when it's not in your best interests.

Both the men and the women began to nod as they got a new view of both themselves and the other side.

THE ALLURE OF THE "BAD BOY," EXPLAINED

The energy was humming in the room when we brought the men and women back together. They sized each other up almost as though they were seeing each other for the first time—and realized how much they'd had wrong before, how much they'd been missing. "Here's your chance," I told them. "Ask anything you want to know about the opposite sex. Ladies? What do you want to know? Guys?"

An expectant silence settled over the group, but no one raised a hand, so I got things rolling with a question that lays bare what happens when chemistry rules dating.

"Okay, ladies," I said. "You all say you want a nice guy. But you go home with the bad guy. Can you help me understand that?"

Silence. No one among the forty women was yelling, "That's not true." There were a few giggles, but no theories, so I helped them along. The bad boy's allure, I explained, went back to safety, and the logic the cavewoman body/brain uses to determine who's capable of protecting her.

Though almost every woman will tell you that she wants a man who puts her first, when he does so in their first interactions, instincts she may not be aware of tend to read his consideration as weakness. The bad guy—the one who gets her quickly into bed, won't call, and seems to care most about himself—paradoxically makes her feel safer. Why? He's in charge. He clearly will take care of himself come what may. A woman sees that and her instincts read it as proof he can protect her too. With behavior that says, "I know what I want, I know where I'm going, and I don't care whether you come along or not," he signals: "I'm the alpha male."

That's one of the crazy aspects of chemistry-driven dating. We say we want one thing, but our instincts respond to something completely different. Guys will say they want to date a woman who's not sleeping around—but she should be sexually experienced. And women swear they want the nice guy, but keep falling for the bad ones. Neither side finds the deep connection they really want. As I explained this, heads nodded all over the room.

What to do? My best advice—and Armstrong's, and Deida's—is this: Learn ways to put your instincts on hold while you connect all the other parts of yourself and give them a voice in the process.

I'm not saying date people you're not attracted to. But build some time into the process to get past the quick "sex or reject" impulse that the chemistry filter dictates.

Think about the people in your life you're closest to, the ones with whom you have the deepest, most real relationships. How did you get to know them? Did you feel a pull, an OMG chemistry? That happens once in a while, sure, but most often there's just a casual, no-fireworks encounter. Some part of your brain just says, "She seems nice." You meet someone on a Habitat for Humanity project or at church or get introduced when you're with a group of friends and slowly start doing things together.

Both of you get to open up about yourselves in a no-pressure way that feels safe, and there's no threat. Instinct isn't in charge, so all the parts of you are there, and you have a genuine chance to connect.

The world, particularly the dating world, is fast-paced—but real connection is slow. Some people do get struck by lightning, but even there, to get from infatuation to intense connection takes time. People often say that if you're friends with someone, you're doomed not to have them as a partner. But I don't see it that way. Friendship builds connection, connection builds intimacy, and that can catch fire, especially if you understand what lights the match.

To get and keep the sparks flying between a man and a woman in a relationship requires maintaining the balance of masculine and feminine, Deida says. In today's world, that often means making sure that the masculine need to be decisive and lead is complemented by the feminine's pleasure in not having to steer the ship all the time. In truth, couples shift roles all the time—no one calls the shots all the time, or wants to. The trick is to be sure that there's one willing leader, not two competing ones, and that both people aren't in the feminine mode of saying, "Anything's fine. You choose."

This can be tough when a woman has played a masculine role all day as a boss at work and has trouble shifting gears when she gets home. Or when husband and wife try to "out-nice" and accommodate each other. None of this is bad, but it can contribute to erasing the polarity between men and women. And it's the contrast, even the friction, between masculine and feminine that amplifies the sexual energy. Take that away, and you've got two pals, with no sexual tension, and no magnetic connection.

For men, a key way to give women what they really want—both consideration and a sense that the masculine is there to reinforce their sense of safety—is to ditch the advice to "be a nice guy" by making your own passions second to those of the woman you desire, and instead to prioritize and feed your own mission in life.

The feminine doesn't trust a pushover, and will test and test the masculine to be sure that it has the power to protect both itself and her. Guys, this means that women don't get easier. They may test (read: complain or fight about) your determination to do things without them or to put in the time you need to go after what you want. And that's fine. Be kind, be generous and be loving—but know that often, love looks like being true to yourself as you help your partner stay true to her own purpose.

Armstrong's advice for women is surprisingly similar. What really turns men on? she asks. It's a woman's passions, be they for career, crocheting, rock climbing, or saving the world. Her sexiest attributes are her self-confidence. Her authenticity—that word again. And her willingness to receive not only what a man has to offer but who he really is. When she's lit from within by her connection with what she loves, and when her eyes light up to see a man she genuinely and lovingly accepts, Armstrong believes a woman becomes irresistible. I heartily second that.

"I'M INDEPENDENT. I DON'T NEED YOU."

Sometimes it seems as though there's not much room for vulnerability and acceptance in the dating world. People long to care for each other and be taken care of, but social roles have changed massively since World War II, when women figured out they could sling rivets and master the workplace as well as any man. It was thrilling. Women wanted equality, and they made great strides toward it.

But in the process, as intimacy coach Karen Brody writes, all of us got something we didn't bargain for: Sameness. Women sometimes felt compelled to reach for power suits with shoulder pads and to force the flowing nature of their creativity into the linear plans and structures built by men. Being equal was often translated as "being more like a man" and "being independent of men."

But the personal cost of doing that can be steep. As we saw in workplace settings earlier in the book, when women feel they have to push down their feminine energy, they sacrifice what sustains them most deeply. They cut themselves off from the essential feminine core that makes them who they are.

In personal relationships, the dynamics can shift dramatically when women begin to equate strength and independence with embodying the masculine, and neglect or play down their feminine essence. The masculine thrives on being able to provide for the feminine and make it happy, but men can feel as though there's nowhere to go, nothing to do, when women are saying, "Oh, don't bother. I've got it covered." Many women today were raised by mothers and fathers who impressed on them that it was important not to have to depend on a man. And that comes across loud and clear in online dating profiles, where the message women inadvertently send the men they're seeking is: "I don't need you." There's something a little odd and counterproductive about that.

On the Internet radio program *Life Bites* not long ago, host Nina Boski and I read women's dating profiles from a popular dating site and had to laugh at the drumbeat of "I don't need you" we found. "I have my own career, friends and lifestyle, and I'm not looking for a guy to take care of me," many of them said, in so many words. "I'm not high-maintenance, I'm *no*-maintenance. I don't want a sugar daddy. I don't want your money. I don't need to hang out with your circle of friends—I've got my own."

The question for a potential partner became: Then why do you need me?

A guy encountering that wall of "I don't need you's tells himself, "Okay. She's a lawyer, making good money. She probably wants a guy who's got an income in the stratosphere. She's got her whole life together. Why would she even be interested in what I've got to offer? I'm not setting myself up to be slapped down."

Women assume that "I don't need you" means "I'll be an equal, not a burden." But what it tells a man is "I won't be able to accept what you have to give." And on a primal level, that douses any potential spark. It may even attract the wrong guy.

Molly Lyda talks about how important it is for women, independent as they are, to step back and make room for what men have to offer. One simple example involves listening. Women are often frustrated when men don't place the same value on feelings that the feminine does. "But so much depends on how safe a man feels with you," she tells women. That sense of safety might come when a woman sits back and just listens to a man, curbing her impulse to jump in and comment and throw in new topics, as her creative essence pushes her to do. Molly urges women to learn to tune into their partners and "wait for it all to come up and out. Alison Armstrong calls this 'waiting for the well,' where you throw a bucket down and let the rope stretch out, then wait for the water to come up and out," she says. "If you hold space and let men talk, make eye contact, you're more likely to get to the emotions."

Molly stresses how valuable it is for women to rein in their masculine side and give the men they're interested in the chance to take an active role in dating. She tells the story of a client who met a man she liked a lot on an online dating site. They went out five or six times, with Molly's client suggesting activity after activity—"This looks great. Want to go?"

But the client began to feel uncomfortable, worrying that she liked the man better than he liked her. He seemed to be pulling away a little. When he sent a text saying, "Why don't you let me move ahead with this," she thought he was saying good-bye and wanted to move on. But further texting revealed what he really wanted to say: "I'd love it if you would take a step back so I can pursue you my way."

The woman did, trusting him to make plans, trusting that she didn't have to engage her masculine side to make something happen. He was asking her to please let him take the lead and give for a while, while she received. When she did, the relationship blossomed.

My best advice for a woman looking for a partner online is to think beyond what she *doesn't* need from a man and to tell the men reading her profile what she *does* want and need. She could start by talking about what she loves about men and how they make her feel. That requires vulnerability, I know, but it would not only connect her potential partners to the truth of who she is, it would invite connection instead of instantly raising a man's defenses.

DAVID GIULIANO

This is not all the responsibility of the woman. Men need to do their part and step up by talking about what they love about women instead of striking a pose and trying to create a shiny, flawless, pumped-up surface. It helps, too, to be real. There's room to talk not just about your job and possessions, but about your real passions, past, and even bad habits. Remember: Chicks dig scars.

My other piece of basic advice for men: Test your assumptions. Rather than thinking that a woman's "I have a great career" means "I will sneer at you if you don't make a brain surgeon's salary and drive a Jaguar," offer her a taste of your genuine, decisive self. Just for laughs, assume that she'll respond to not having to "be the man" and make all the decisions for a change. Instead of retreating, take the risk of engaging, and leading, on a date. Her openness to that may surprise you.

There's one good thing about the "I don't need you" dilemma: It gives us a good reason to go back and look at the basics. What *do* we want in our love relationships, anyway?

TRY IT YOURSELF: WHAT DO YOU
REALLY WANT IN RELATIONSHIPS?

To help people keep their focus on that question—What *do* we really want in relationships?—Molly and I followed up with our retreat group three months later and asked just a handful of questions, which you may want to ask yourself:

– What do you want from men?

– What do you want to create *with* them?

– What do you want from women?

– What do you want to create *with* them?

It's interesting to see how the perspective shifts when you move from thinking about what you want from someone to what you want to create with them. I think it's important to look from the very personal vantage point of "What do I want to receive?" But it's revealing to then look through the eyes of the relationship itself,

146

and think about how you'd like things to be when you are part of a unit called "us."

Answering these questions may be harder than you realize—which was definitely the case for me. The first time someone asked me what I wanted from a woman, it caught me off guard, and truthfully I didn't have a good answer. Of course there were the basics that we all say we have to have—I wanted her to be smart and good-looking, sexy and honest—but to get to the answers that help you connect with someone who's a genuine match, you have to look at a much deeper level. As I slowed down to think about what I really wanted, I suddenly realized that at age fifty-plus, I still wasn't clear. And when clarity started to come, I saw that my answers had changed drastically from my old assumptions.

Without getting into the details, the answers were profound for me. (Picture thinking you could only fall for a young, blonde bombshell and realizing that you're actually most attracted to rumpled women who laugh a lot, and come with kids and dogs.) I came away with a new understanding and an openness to much wider possibilities. I also pointed myself clearly away from what I no longer wanted or needed.

I highly recommend this exercise. Let your imagination open your heart and mind, and dream up your ideal partner. Try not to overthink it, and most of all, have fun.

THERE ARE MANY WAYS TO CONNECT, SO PICK A PARTNER WHO WANTS WHAT YOU WANT

For much of my life, I assumed that there was one reason to want a relationship: to give and receive love. In her book, *The Gifts of Imperfection*, Brené Brown writes: "We cultivate love when we allow our most vulnerable and powerful selves to be deeply seen and known, and when we honor the spiritual connection that grows from that offering with trust, respect, kindness and affection."

That's my ideal, and my automatic response to those words is: Who would not want to put that kind of big, authentic love at the center of a relationship?

But I've come to see that relationships are built on a much wider variety of foundations, all of them valid, and all potentially the basis for connection—as long as you both know and agree about what you want and value most.

Alison Armstrong talks about four broad relationship categories, and I find them to be helpful. "Legacy" relationships are about a desire for kids or for carrying on a family line, a heritage, or a tradition. A "companionship" model is one in which a pair of low-key partners might choose each other because they get along and like to do things together. In "support" relationships, each partner helps the other reach cherished dreams. Her final model, the "karma" relationship, is about each person challenging the other to expand themselves in all ways, physical, emotional, and spiritual.

A guy who's looking for friendly companionship and comfort from a woman might assume that his partner will be fulfilled by that too, only to find later that her real desire was for kids, or personal growth, or passion. Knowing what you want, and being clear about what the other person expects, will save you much heartache.

WHY "I LOVE YOU" MAY NOT BE ENOUGH

I'm a big fan of the discussions that happen in a process called Pre-Cana in the Catholic church, where engaged couples spend a weekend answering questions about their needs and expectations to be sure they're on the same page. The topics get as basic as "Why do you want to be with each other?" and couples are asked to be very specific about the roles each person expects to play. The goal is to be sure that everyone is signing up for the same version of marriage, and that there's no shocked moment when Mr. "I thought you'd have three meals on the table for me every day" realizes his partner doesn't like to cook. The best marriages will have thousands of unforeseen challenges—that's just life. So it makes sense to be sure you won't be blindsided by issues that can be easy to identify at the outset by stepping outside of your feelings and getting clear about what's really important to each of you.

We also delve into the spiritual aspects of a partnership, openly discussing what's most valued, including what each person most values about the other. When I facilitate these sessions, I remind people that in long-term relationships there will be rough spots, and it can be extremely valuable to go back to their original answers, especially to see what lit them up about each other at the beginning, before the mortgage, four kids, twenty pounds, and credit card debt got in the way. The clarity you establish early on can guide, inspire you along the way, and remind you of who you are as a couple. You don't have to do this formally, or in a religious context, but as you build intimacy with someone, you can have conversations that let both of you know who you really are, and what you want.

Hearkening back to the Grid from chapter 3, you could use a question like "What do we most want to see/hear/be aware of in our future life together?" to wander into a vision of the fantasies and dreams you'd like to make real.

It's not for an outsider to understand a relationship, or to say you should want any particular kind. People often compare themselves to others, or look at couples and wonder what in the heck made them want to marry. But that's one of the mysteries of love. I've seen countless relationships that I don't understand. And that's fine. It's not for me to understand. The only arbiters of whether a relationship makes sense and is working are the people involved. The rest of us can only guess.

ME/WE/THEE

I had a great "aha!" moment when my men's group was introduced to the idea that relationships tend to fall into three broad categories—Me, We, and Thee. It can be extremely difficult to see a relationship from inside its habits and dramas, and I've found it useful to use these categories as a reference to help me think about how I'm showing up in a relationship, and what kinds of assumptions are in play. The categories are descriptions, not judgments. A good relationship is one that meets the needs of both parties—

we get to set the terms, and at different times in our lives, we may want completely different sorts of interaction with our partners. My intention here isn't to label your relationship, but to make it easier for you to be conscious of what you have, and what you might want to create.

A **"ME" RELATIONSHIP** revolves around the question: "What's in it for me?" It's more about getting than giving, and it tends to lack emotional connection. While it can work if the partners manage to do their taking from each other without incurring resentments, it can be fairly lonely, because there's not a lot of heart involved. If you're in a Me relationship, chances are that parts of you are shut down.

I find that people in Me relationships aren't always conscious that they've created a dynamic that revolves around their own needs, and they often wonder why the other person is pulling away. I'll sometimes hear a friend complaining about how his girlfriend is unhappy with him, fighting with him about things he wants to do, calling him selfish. "What's her problem? How is it selfish that I'm setting up all these things and wanting to take her places?" he'll ask, going on to describe what a pain it is when his partner resists going along with his plans, friends, and agendas.

"But what's in it for her?" I might ask. "Does she like any of this stuff? Did you ask her about it?" Sometimes it's as though he's so used to making plans the way he did when he was single that he hasn't really considered that he must now take another person's feelings into account. She has needs of her own, and would appreciate his empathy and attention. In longer-term relationships, sometimes the Me emphasis comes from taking the other person for granted, or getting so swept up in your own stresses or enthusiasms that you forget to connect.

"WE" RELATIONSHIPS, the kind most of us have, are built on love, affection, and, many times, on some kind of unconscious agreement about what each person will give and get. In visualizing themselves as a We, people naturally look at the puzzle of their lives and imagine the gaps their partnering will fill, noticing the parts that will mesh and complement one another.

Sometimes expectations are set at the outset: I'll be the funny one, and you'll be the one who laughs at my jokes. Or, I'll be the strong one, and you'll be the one who needs mending. We connect around security, family, opportunity, companionship, adventure, to name just a few—and often it's not hard to see the agreement operating in the background: "I'll take care of the house and kids if you'll pay the bills," or "I'll put you through school if you use your MD to support me while I write my novel."

In the strongest We relationships, both people understand what's wanted, needed, and expected on both sides. They also allow each other to change, renegotiating roles and even identities over time. When the kids are gone, when the "strong" partner hits hard times, when a strange and wonderful mission calls, old understandings need to become new ones. A healthy We is dynamic, and when it's not, tensions, disappointments, and even feelings of betrayal can build, and seem to erupt out of nowhere. Without flexibility and clear communication, even a close We relationship can slip into a Me, and connection can falter or break. But with careful tending, a We is big enough to hold all the joy and challenges of long-term love.

THE "THEE" RELATIONSHIP is built from a generous, even selfless, state of consciousness. What it values most highly is the full and authentic expression of each person's gifts. Partners in a Thee relationship say, "I am here to love and support you in your highest good and on your path. And you are here to support me in my highest good on my path. I see God in you. I acknowledge the divine in you. I take you to God in the way I love you."

It's perhaps on the order of Armstrong's "karmic" relationship, with both partners honoring and helping the other achieve their purpose in life.

Partners in a Thee relationship respect each other, want the best for each other, and weather the unknowns that surface when the goal is authenticity, not safety, and they enter the vulnerable space of not being able to predict what will happen. That means a Thee relationship isn't a magical fairy-tale coupling in which things are always good and the partners are always on the same path, happily ever after. A Thee relationship doesn't join people at the hip. They most likely do things separately, perhaps even for long periods when their dreams ask them to go different directions to try or experiment with something new.

The bittersweet knowledge at the center of Thee is that the forces pulling the other person toward what means the most to her or him may pull the couple apart. The love a Thee relationship flows from is unconditional. It wants the best for the other, even when that may bring the pain of separation or loss. It's far from easy, but it rewards those who experience it with profound joy, acceptance, and transformation.

Most healthy relationships have elements of We and Thee, and occasional lapsing into Me isn't unheard of. The important thing to keep in mind is that *you* are the one who chooses the kind of relationship you want. With your own openness, you can let partners or potential partners know what level of intimacy and connection you want.

LOVE IS NOT LINEAR OR LOGICAL.
IT DOESN'T ALWAYS WORK OUT
THE WAY YOU WANT. LOVE ANYWAY.

Whatever kind of love you want, and whatever you think love is, the thing to keep in mind is that love doesn't care. It's a force we can't control, much as we'd like to, and the point of staying open to it is that when we do, we can go along for the ride, and see what love has in mind for us. What I can tell you with absolute certainty is that the experience will be worth it. If you haven't had your heart broken at least once, you haven't lived.

Loving, and staying open to love, is what we're here to do as men and women. We love because we're human, and because we're spiritual beings, connecting not just with each other but also with something much larger.

There's no way to do love wrong, because there's nothing perfect about it—it's not *supposed* to be perfect.

A while back, I wrote a poem/prayer/reflection that aims to get at all this, and I'd like to share it with you now, as you're thinking about what it will take to stay open to another person, and what could happen when you do. Feel free to add your own thoughts and experiences with love. I wish you all that love has to teach you.

Love Doesn't Care

We try to control it, but that's not meant to be.

Love is changing constantly.

The deeper we love, the more vulnerable we become.

Love opens us. Love closes us. That's the way of love.

Love leaves us. Love waits for us. Love leads us. Love
grounds us.

Love bends us, love breaks us, love molds us. Love takes
us.

Love brings us back, brings us to our knees,

Love blinds us. Love brings us clarity.

Love pushes when we need to move, makes us grow
without choice,

Love makes music, makes us silent, love speaks in our
own voice.

Love makes us laugh, love makes us cry.

Love makes us leave. It makes us stay.

Love makes us fight. It makes us play.

Love makes us wrong. It makes us right.

Love makes us feel so alive, makes us feel we want to die.

Love scares us, tears us apart,
Love chooses us. Love leaves us.
Love waits for us. It leads us. Love connects us. Love
   needs us.
Love preaches. Love teaches.
Love makes us mean. It makes us clean.
Love makes us pray.
Love makes us love.
And so we love.
It's never the same.
It's never perfect—it's not meant to be.
Amen.

CHAPTER 7

Keeping Connection
Strong in Love Relationships

Though I'm not a counselor or therapist, my business coaching practice and friendships sometimes seem like a lab for watching the power of connection play out in love relationships. As I listen to the stories of clients and friends, I can't help but notice that just as we've seen in business scenarios, the challenge in our relationships is to stay connected when conflicts, distance, or change begin to unsettle us.

In this chapter, I'd like to show you the way the connection skills and tools we used for business can help love relationships run more smoothly. I've often seen that people come at relationship stresses and problems in a more creative, open way when they first focus on basic connection—staying connected to the authentic self and what it knows, connecting to what's best about the other person, and connecting to the vision of "us at our best" that was there at the beginning.

Focusing on connection alone isn't enough to help you repair a broken, toxic, or abusive relationship, or face deep-seated issues with fear, trust, or intimacy—for that, you'll want the expertise of a therapist. But the skills we'll talk about in this chapter can enhance relationships that are standing on solid ground. By that I mean relationships in which there may be pain, doubt, a little jealousy, and some insecurity, but where there's also faith, an open heart, deep love, great respect, vulnerability, and a willingness to keep going through the pain and doubt.

I think of the kind of troubles that come to these sorts of relationships as "good hard," and that's the "level of difficulty" we'll be navigating in the sections that follow.

THE DISTANCE BETWEEN THEN AND NOW

Whether I'm coaching a business or talking to a friend who's having a problem with a spouse, I always go back to a fundamental truth: You know what a powerful connection looks like with this person or situation, because you've experienced it. When the relationship started, you were passionate about the possibilities, and dazzled by the appeal of the other party and what they brought into your world. The relationship was built on that attraction; it was the foundation from which everything developed.

So when difficulty arises, I suggest to people that they go back to the beginning and try to look through the eyes that saw the relationship when it was new.

It's a great experiment to try any time you want to reinforce your connection with another person, and it's a powerful starting point for untangling stubborn relationship issues.

TRY IT YOURSELF: GOING
BACK TO THE BEGINNING

These questions can lead you back to the memory of when times were good. Reflecting on them will help bring you clarity about what you want and where you stand now. Ask:

- What was it like when you were madly in love?

- What's the difference between then and now?

- What was happening then?

- What attracted you to your partner? What worked really well between you?

- What do you feel you're losing now?

- How far away are you now from what you wish you had?

- What's the difference between who you are now and who you were then?

It can be empowering to remember what made the relationship so satisfying. You knew what it took to make it spark and sizzle—and you still do. The elements are all there in your longing for what's missing, and once you see them in front of you, you can, if you're willing to take the risk of closeness, share them with your partner. Origin stories—the details of what brought two people together—have a power that never ceases to surprise me.

TELLING OLD STORIES TO CREATE A NEW ONE

My friends Kylie and J.B. had hit a "good hard" patch in their marriage, and we sat talking about it one weekend. (This is a composite story based on real conversations, with names and details changed to protect everyone's privacy.) Kylie was a nurse when she met J.B., and he's a network administrator. Kylie loves to tell the story of how they met on a blind date at a bowling alley. "I'd never bowled before in my life. But he took us over to a funky little place and we had the time of our lives. I slipped and fell down the first time I tried to get the ball down the lane, and we always say that's when I fell for him, too."

Kylie quit her job when the twins came, and for years now she's been a full-time mom, getting up at dawn to get the kids fed and dressed, and then manage the homework, carpool, and team duties that come up for two active boys. J.B. also felt like he'd been running nonstop. "I don't know if I ever quite recovered from the shock of having two kids—double trouble—at once," he said with a wry smile. "I feel like a big wave swept in and we not only had a mortgage, but tuition to think about, and all the things that kids need. Plus Kylie couldn't really work. So I've been working my butt off ever since."

It's clear from the way they looked at each other that the love was still there, but they were candid about the layers of busyness and creeping resentments that were getting in the way.

"I love being a mom," Kylie said, and it's clear she does. "But I had no idea what I was signing up for. I can't tell you the last time I just sat down and read a book, or touched my piano, or had a minute to myself. I'm just going nuts, and I'm so tired, I'm nothing but complaints and orders when J.B. gets home. I miss having alone time. Sometimes I feel like I can't keep this up for much longer."

"It's crazy, hon," J.B. said. "I miss that funny girl I took bowling! What ever happened to her?"

He reached over and squeezed her hand, and we sipped our coffee, quiet.

"I want to do your questions," Kylie said after a while. She and J.B. had heard me talking about a relationships workshop where I'd mentioned going back to the beginning of a couple's story to find the way forward. "How does that go again? I want to try it if you and J.B. are game."

Our friendship is close and open, and J.B. was willing, so I talked them through a bit of the list.

"The basic format sounds like this," I said. "You'd say something like: 'Honey, I know things have been tough for us lately, and both of us have been unhappy. But I want to tell you why I fell in love with you. When I met you [xyz] is how we connected. You were [like this], and I was [like this], and I was so wild about you. Do you remember that? Do you remember how we [did xyz]?' You fill in the blanks with details. The xyzs would be about bowling and whatever else you want to talk about. I've heard you two. I know you have a lot of details."

J.B. talked not just about the intrepid girl he met who fell down bowling and got up laughing. He remembered the way Kylie lit up talking about her work in the geriatrics ward during nursing school.

Kylie talked about falling in love with a guy who kept whisking her off on hikes and adventures and who was full of funny stories about the people he worked with and helped.

Their smiles were warm and genuine as they spoke, even as both said wistfully that they hadn't seen those laughing, impassioned sides of themselves in years. Remembering and reconnecting with who you were at the beginning isn't about saying that change is bad, I reminded them, and it's not about going back to that time in your lives—you can't. But feeling the connection again gives you a path to what's best in you, and that can pull you closer.

EASING INTO THE TOUGH STUFF

Sometimes just that—just remembering who you are as a couple in love with each other—can restore a sputtering connection. Most often though, there's more to address, and it's much easier to do with the warmth that you create when you tell your partner, "This is why I fell in love with you."

Because I'm a friend of both J.B. and Kylie, I knew that J.B. had been shouldering the burden of his anxieties about finances alone. "Kylie has enough to worry about," he told me. "I can't bring home the office politics and rumors that are giving me an ulcer."

But from a distance, I'd been watching a familiar relationship pattern play out. Holding in his worries made J.B. pull away—secrets naturally put distance between us and the ones we're keeping in the dark. Kylie sensed that, and began worrying that he was hiding something, or that something had gone wrong between them.

HE KEEPS A SECRET, SHE PICKS A FIGHT: A CLASSIC RELATIONSHIP TANGO

When this "he pulls away/she suspects trouble" dynamic is set in motion, a woman no longer feels safe, and she often feels abandoned. Her response: She picks a fight, in part because of the stress and frustration, and in part because it might be a way to drag the truth into the light. That's the pattern: Stress builds in the male partner's life. He avoids talking about it, creating distance in the relationship that scares the female partner. And the fighting begins.

Avoidance drains authenticity from people and relationships, and as it continues, feelings get repressed, resentments and fears build, and connections get fuzzier and fuzzier because so much is unspoken and kept hidden.

Creating or restoring real connection in relationships, for men in particular, means working to overcome the tendency to avoid uncomfortable truths and feelings. Men like to heal by isolating—going back to the man cave, out to the garage, and sometimes they can get more clarity there. But they need to bring that clarity back to their partner, because avoidance is where trouble starts. You withhold the truth from your partner, and soon you become afraid to tell yourself the truth, too. And now you've compounded the original worry with a bigger one: Your relationship is falling apart.

THE ISSUE OF SAFETY

It made me uncomfortable to see that happening between my friends, and since we were all together, I asked if they were interested in helping me with a little relationship research. "I've been teaching a lot about safety in man/woman relationships, and I want to try out one of the big ideas on you. Are you game?"

They both nodded.

"Okay, here's a question for you, J.B. How safe would you say you feel with Kylie? How safe is the relationship?"

He looked at me like I was crazy. "Safe? Of course it's safe."

"Okay," I said. "Let me ask you this: Do you feel safe enough to tell the person you're closest to in your life how you feel about everything?"

His pained look said more than any words could have.

I looked at Kylie and asked her if she shared her feelings with J.B. in the same direct way she talked about them with her female friends. Again, I got the "Are you crazy?!" look.

"You know how guys are, David. You all don't like to talk about feelings, and I think you guys can be even more sensitive than a woman," she said. "I don't want to force the issue."

Honesty between men and women requires navigating some tricky primal territory. The masculine, primed to protect the feminine, believes that a woman will panic if confronted with the real vulnerability that surfaces when a man says, "We're in a financial bind," or "I just got a bad diagnosis from the doctor." Many men have concluded that the upset and fear their honesty can create only makes things worse. And many women tacitly say, "Just do what you need to do—take care of it and let me know when things are all better again."

But the thing about intimacy is that it can only grow in the presence of openness and trust. It demands vulnerability. If you're my partner and I don't take the risk of telling you what I think and want and need because I'm worried that you'll get upset or you "can't deal with feelings," then intimacy just isn't going to happen. That can leave both parties feeling isolated and lonely.

I suggested to J.B. that a middle ground for him could be to sort out his raw feelings with male friends, instead of dumping them unfiltered on Kylie, but then to quickly bring the truth home to her. It makes both the masculine and the feminine relax when the masculine can offer the leadership of a good next step, even if it's not the one you ultimately take. When the instincts let down their guard, it's easier to connect and problem-solve together.

"I think I can handle it all," Kylie told J.B. "Let's talk about it. I promise I won't freak out. You can probably deal with more honesty from me too," she said, squeezing his hand.

To start, I said, I'd e-mail some ground rules that help bring a sense of safety to deep conversations that feel risky not because they're threatening, but because they bring hidden truths into the open and can leave each party feeling exposed.

GROUND RULES FOR IMPORTANT CONVERSATIONS

We all assume that people should be able to carry on the important conversations in their lives without anything so formal as rules, but I find that whether I'm helping business clients negotiate or talking through issues with friends, there's something freeing about the neutral, open environment that these guidelines help create. J.B. and Kylie both texted back to say how valuable this structure quickly proved to be.

FIRST, MAKE THE SPACE EMOTIONALLY SAFE. Many conversations don't go anywhere because the parties feel as though they could be sniped, attacked, or ridiculed if they make themselves vulnerable by being honest. Safety can mean, "I want to be able to tell you my real feelings without your running out the door." It can mean, "Let me finish what I have to say," or "I need to know that I can finish, even if you start to cry. Your tears can't trump my truth."

ASK THE OTHER PERSON WHAT HE OR SHE NEEDS TO MAKE THE SPACE FEEL SAFE, AND THINK ABOUT WHAT YOU NEED. If you're talking about volatile topics, or if one person feels especially fearful, it helps to have a third person, someone who won't be affected by the outcome, guiding or containing the situation. A coach or therapist can be a good choice, a neutral party who can help ensure that each party has a chance to speak fully and freely.

CREATE A STRUCTURE FOR THE CONVERSATION. I like to put a ground rule in place that says: "Each person will listen without interrupting, defending, or objecting." Agree that you'll let each other say what you have to say. That doesn't mean you have license to attack each other. It means speaking with respect and remaining as open as you can.

USE ACTIVE LISTENING. I had an unforgettable lesson in listening a dozen years ago when I found myself in a difficult situation with a girlfriend. She asked if I'd go to a therapy session with her to talk about our differences, and when I got there, the therapist said, "We're going to do an exercise called 'active listening.'"

"Great," I said. "I'm a fantastic listener!"

Active listening, the therapist explained, consists of listening to the other person speak, then repeating back or paraphrasing what he or she just said. If the other person says, "I would appreciate it if you'd only wear yellow clothes, because they cheer me up." You, as the active listener, say, "I heard you say that you want me to just wear yellow, because it cheers you up."

That seemed simple enough. Needless to say, I failed miserably. After my girlfriend spoke the first seven or eight words, my brain jumped to defending my position, and I almost literally went deaf. All I could repeat back, on my first few tries, were those initial words, and after that, I absorbed nothing. I realized that that's what always happened when my girlfriend and I fought—I'd stop listening so I could work on my defense.

Both men and women want to feel heard and understood, and active listening is a vehicle for reinforcing that feeling. In these exchanges, it's not a woman's responsibility to manage her man's pain. It's not a man's responsibility to jump in to fix a woman's problem, or to do anything but be there for her, listening. Using active listening helps everyone stay in the present, paying attention to what's being said, not planning what to do about it.

The speaker's main responsibility is to be truthful. It's not productive for anyone to dump their problems and issues on the other person and blame him or her. Connection and solutions will come when each side is finally able to tell his or her truths.

KEEP RETURNING TO
THE CONNECTION WITH THE SELF

As J.B. and Kylie pulled their fears and hopes out of hiding, they told me, they talked at length about being "people as well as parents," as Kylie put it. They both loved parenthood, but the obligations and pressures that came with their twins had caused a separation, because as their new responsibilities consumed them, neither could be the person the other fell in love with. For the best of reasons, they had lost touch with important parts of themselves, and they couldn't be authentic again—or reestablish their connection with each other—until they reconnected with the things that fed their core. I'd done some work with J.B. in his business, and I suggested that he teach Kylie some of what he'd learned about re-connecting with the authentic self.

Both of them had talked about wanting time—time for them-selves, when they could be someone besides "Mommy" or "Mr. 24/7 I.T. Guy" and enjoy both their own company and each other's. It was urgent to find a way to do that again, because the farther they moved from their authentic selves, the more they were unknowingly pushing each other away.

But what would it look like to have more balance in their lives? "I can't even imagine it," Kylie told me over the phone.

J.B. told me later that he'd pulled out his New Knowing Grid and suggested to Kylie that they use it to get more specific about what they wanted their lives to look like.

"I just showed her the 'Imagining' column, and it really ap-pealed to her," he said. "She imagined creating an opening in her life where she was just Kylie, not Mom or Mrs. J.B. or chauffeur or PTA mom or anything else. We did the whole thing aloud. It was great. I told her that first she should listen for what she wanted to be hearing in her Kylie life. If it was a perfect day, and she was just being Kylie, what would she hear?

"She said music. There would be lots of music. She would be playing the piano, and we'd be dancing in the kitchen while we made dinner with the stereo blaring. I forgot we used to do that! She just looked so happy as she was talking. And we were both going, we could make that happen. Oh, and she also heard some-thing else: Someone calling her name on a hospital PA. She had this flash of being back at work. That was a surprise. We're both still thinking about that.

"The vision part was less vivid for her. But in the New Knowing part, she just said she knew that she didn't have to give up every-thing to be a mom. It wasn't either/or. She said she wanted to give up 'knowing' that she had do everything for the kids and not have time for herself. And I promised to help her find a way."

For himself, J.B. said, he was surprised to blurt out to Kylie that what he longed to hear was "wind in the pines. It was a sound I remember from being in the woods with my father," he told me, "and I had this vision of being out camping with the boys. We've never done that, but we could. I think they'd like it."

You can use different parts of the Grid to gain clarity about what's really going on with you, what kind of deals you've made with yourself, and what's aching to be done or expressed. It's a good window into the past, as well as the future. And as J.B. noticed, using the Grid as a vehicle for conversation can bring you closer to your partner. For the first time in a long time, you might be talking about your dreams.

TRANSLATING DESIRES INTO A PLAN WITHOUT SHAME

When Kylie excitedly asked me for suggestions about getting more music, and maybe even nursing, into her life again, I told her about the Not To Do list you saw in chapters 1 and 2, which J.B. had done in business coaching. Owning where you are can sometimes feel painful, and I reminded her that this process is not about shaming yourself. It's about saying, "Point A is where I am now, and Point B is where I want to be." As we've seen, making a Not To Do list is a way of owning your real feelings and communicating a message that's much deeper than, "I don't want to drive the kids to soccer every weekend anymore." You're also saying, "I've been inauthentic until now. And because I haven't communicated what I need, you don't know. I've been living a lie because I was too afraid to tell you the truth. I'm telling you this because I want you to know me. Let's figure out how to make a change." This is important enough to say aloud to your partner, especially the words: "I want you to know who I really am." That can create an intimate connection.

The No. 1 item on Kylie's Not To Do list was getting the boys ready for bed every night. "If I just had a few nights when I could go down to the basement and practice the piano while you read them stories, I would feel so much more human," she told J.B.

J.B. wanted to change their nighttime routine, too. "I know we've always watched *The Tonight Show* in bed," he said, "but I want to use that time do some reading—I don't know the last time I finished a novel. You talked about reading too. We can do it together, even read the same book so we can talk about it."

The give and take, adjustments and honesty started there, and in time they worked up to bigger issues, like seeing if the kids' grandparents could watch them a day a week so Kylie could get her hand back in nursing and ease the financial strain on J.B.

These conversations can feel scary, especially when they involve changing a longtime routine, or finally saying no to something that you've been resentfully going along with for years. Any kind of change takes adjustment, and can feel threatening, but you can talk your way through it and build closeness with your honesty. You may not love your partner's request, but look at it this way: If you truly love someone, and see them for who they are, do you really want them to do things that make them unhappy every day?

TALK ABOUT WHAT YOU DO WANT

J.B. called me one night to ask if I had any suggestions for talking to Kylie about things he hoped she might do for him, little touches that had been part of their relationship before the boys were born, and that he'd been missing.

"We're on this good track now, and I don't want to blow it," he said. "I just think things could be even better."

I suggested that he try going back to that original list of questions he and Kylie started out with. "There's a part that goes like this," I said. "You each fill in the details in the statement: 'This is what I'm missing about you, about us, and this is what I need and want to have with you now.'" Those are gentle words, and they help keep the conversation as loving as it is direct.

Here's a hint: It works best to start with a positive when you're doing this. In other words, say something like: "I really loved it when you used to give me a big hug and a kiss when I got home from work. I've been missing that so much. It would make me so happy if we could start doing that again."

Feel the difference between those words and these: "You never give me a hug and a kiss anymore when I get home. I want that again." Framed like that, a request can sound like a complaint, an accusation, or a whine—and all of those put your partner on the defensive. Consciously start with the positive and remind your partner of how it felt to do the things you miss: "Remember when we used to have those crazy date nights and go to the drive-in or try ice cream places at the beach? I love being with you like that and I really miss it. Let's get out the calendar and make a date."

Those kinds of clear, loving requests can result in quick, satisfying changes. They did for J.B., who started enjoying the "welcome home" hugs and lunchtime "I'm thinking of you" calls he'd missed so much. The hardest part is articulating them—and that gets easier the more you open up to your partner again. For fun, the two of you might play with the Grid, walking down the Imagine column, and talking through what excites you most now. It's a way to get current with the other person, and let the reality of who she or he is now into your imagination.

WHEN THE TROUBLE IS THE THICKEST, KEEP TALKING

Stuff happens. Job losses. Illness. Every kind of business stress. Trouble with the kids. Clients, particularly men, have nervously told me, "I'm scared. I hate my life and if I could, I'd just walk away." Sometimes that thought, just the thought, is so terrifying that they freeze in place, afraid to do anything. But taking the most frightening thoughts out of your head and speaking them to someone who cares about you is enough to help most people get past the paralysis and into a more active mode.

Articulating what you've been feeling changes the energy because it gives you back a piece of yourself, and liberates all the energy you were putting into hiding, denying, and minimizing your feelings. The more you can be truthful and authentic, the less your fears will control you, and the more inner resources you'll free up for taking positive action in your life.

When you bring more openness to your relationship, you allow it to deepen, and you give your partner a chance to offer help, ideas, and emotional support.

Maintaining the Relationship

Closeness isn't a one-time event. It takes ongoing work to keep your connection with your partner strong, especially in tough times, when it may seem as though there's no time or energy to spare for something as "frivolous" as this.

One example of a positive life event that can be unexpectedly disruptive is when a child is born, and with good reason. A woman's focus shifts from her husband to the baby, and her feminine energy is now directed to the child. The masculine suffers greatly from the loss, and may withdraw, or even respond to nurturing feminine energy elsewhere. But paying attention to each other, even in the throes of stress or disruption, can keep you talking, laughing, connected, in touch—and touching.

Physical connection with the ones we love is one of the best feelings in the world, but we tend to turn away from it when we or our relationships are under stress. The good news is that as you start to reestablish emotional connection with yourself and your partner, physical connection reopens too. You can coax it back in many ways. There's magic in great sex with another person, but don't dismiss the closeness that comes with everyday touch—that hug, the way you catch the other person's eye and caress their cheek, the way you offer a reassuring touch, or hold their hand.

There was a moment earlier in the chapter when my friend J.B reached for his wife Kylie's hand as they were starting to open up about their relationship. It was a very small thing, but it stays with me because I can still see how Kylie's whole body relaxed when J.B.'s big hand enveloped hers. I could tell she felt safe. Physical connection can create a sense of safety that words can't match on their own. Don't underestimate the amazing gift you can give the one you love with even the briefest moment of eye contact and physical connection.

Remembering to communicate with touch again may take effort

at first. Many of us tend to live more in our minds than in our bodies these days, more likely to gaze lovingly at our phones than at our mates. The key to coming back to the body, and back to the habit of touch, is to decide on some simple rituals for connecting and commit to using them. Here are a few that have worked for my clients and friends:

SIMPLE RITUALS FOR REGULAR CONNECTION

- Take ten minutes before bed to check in with yourself and each other. Decide that while you're talking, you'll hold hands or make other physical contact.
- Talk while walking the dog.
- Hire a sitter and go out for breakfast on Saturday morning.
- Go out dancing, or bowling—something physical that you liked to do before you got too busy—once a month.
- Take an hour every couple of days to do something creative or refreshing alone together. A drive. A walk on the beach.
- Hug for a solid minute, morning and night, then talk.

The important thing is to keep talking, listening, touching, asking, and noticing what's going on with the other person. Not the kids, not the business, not the whole rest of life: just your partner.

Learning to be present is an especially rewarding and powerful skill.

There are many other exercises for couples interested in shaking off the details of everyday life and focusing, even briefly, just on each other. To start, simply pick any one of them, any point of connection, and use it.

Women, I should mention, are much better at paying attention to relationships, and to the world in general, than men are. As I've mentioned, their survival depends on it, and it's part of the primal feminine. Women can be incredulous toward men—"How could you not notice xyz?"—but in defense of men, a lot of things just escape us. Books could, and probably should, be written for men on how to pay attention. And women could use volumes on how to communicate without being accusatory or unkind.

The better we understand our natures, the more we can work with them. That's the joy of having two sexes: We can fascinate each other with our differences. The masculine is practical—it wants a problem to solve. The feminine is emotional, and can carry the masculine away with the richness of its imagination.

We need each other. And we find our way back to each other through ourselves. If you're looking for joy in your partner, look for joy in yourself first. As Kylie made time for music, and J.B. let himself remember what it was like to be outside in the wind and pines, their world grew, and the distance that had stretched between them closed up. They were dancing in the kitchen, dancing back into their lives.

CHAPTER 8

Family and Parenting: Passing on the Value of Connection

Imagine that you'd grown up watching your parents build their lives around their authentic selves, teaching you by example what it takes to weave strong connections to yourself, the people you love, and to the world. What difference would that have made in your life?

It might be that you know exactly, because your parents made choices that supported their deepest gifts and passions, and showed you how to do the same.

But many, perhaps most, of us came from families in which pursuing a life's purpose was secondary to survival, and fulfillment wasn't a big part of the conversation. Let me ask you again, though: What would it be like for a child to learn the skills of connection and authenticity as he or she learned to walk or read or drive?

My guess is that it would liberate the kind of joy and creative energy that could transform families, businesses and whole communities, not to get too crazily optimistic about it. So in this chapter, I'd like to share some tools and ideas that can help parents build connection both with and within their children.

It's a vast topic, and I can't begin to cover it completely, but I'll highlight three key elements that allow connection to thrive—presence, respect, and safety—and show how to strengthen them in your children and the kids in your life. We'll look at some of the areas that pose the biggest challenges to parents, and I'll suggest the kinds of choices that can help families create and teach connection, rather than pushing it away.

CONNECTION THRIVES ON PRESENCE

I eat most of my meals in restaurants, and as many people have noted, the atmosphere in every casual dining spot—and even in high-end places—has changed massively since the arrival of the first iPhone in 2007. Once I'd see families come in with toys and crayons for small children, and watch the steady interaction that comes with teaching kids to use their indoor voices, refrain from bopping people at neighboring tables with menus, or keep elbows and feet off the table. But now there's often a strange, still silence. At the first sign of misbehavior, restlessness, or boredom, the screens come out, and I frequently see hushed groups staring into the lulling light of their phones. Sometimes I'll catch the eye of a toddler who was unable to get her mom's attention because Mom was texting or shopping on her phone.

I'm not that cranky guy who thinks everything was better when he was a kid. There are plenty of *Leave It to Beaver*-era rituals and attitudes about family that are best left in the past. But increasingly, I see how difficult it is for parents and kids to connect, because even when they're sitting side by side, technology can easily muscle between them. Neither is fully present to the other.

I'm fully sympathetic to the dad who needs a quick way to appease his crying two-year-old and feels as though he's won the lottery every time he can pull up a distracting app and put it in front of the toddler to get some peace. I understand when people tell me they only way they can go out for brunch with the family without guilt is if they "check in with work" a couple of times. I get it. It was never realistic to think that we could be tuned in 24/7 to our families. We all need to check out once in a while, and to pay attention to the other parts of our lives.

But I think that many of us are way past the point where we check out "once in a while." I notice us turning to our individual screens for company and connection even while we're in the presence of real people—including our children. That means we're regularly missing in-person opportunities to look into their eyes, pick up the tone with which a fourth grader says, "He was mean to me but it's okay," or laugh at a six-year-old's first attempts to tell a joke. There's real disappointment and loneliness in children when their parents are so in the habit of "connecting" with their devices that they don't even look up when a son climbs in the car, excited to talk after soccer practice, or a daughter holds up a paper with a gold star that she's been wanting to show her mom all day. The casual, everyday interactions that bind people together are eroding, say researchers like Sherry Turkle from MIT, and children are suffering from their parent's lack of presence, which they can't make up for by retreating into screens of their own.

Presence means being in your body, paying attention to the other person, making eye contact, listening and responding, picking up the nonverbal cues they're giving, sharing your genuine responses. To be present with your children is to see them, ask questions, notice what they say and do, or offer hugs and the kind of casual touch that says, "You're safe. I'm here. I see you." Presence keeps you connected, even when it seems that a child would rather be playing a game or texting a friend. In demonstrating presence, you're teaching your child what it looks like, and why it's meaningful. You're actually, physically, being there for them.

Raising the level of presence you bring into your family takes work, and I'd be the last person to suggest that if you only put away your phone, everything will be just fine. But I have seen friends and colleagues who wanted to be more conscious of the way they let technology infuse their family life make the choice to put limits on it—with great success. That's why tech cutbacks are among my suggestions for strengthening the amount of presence you and your family make available to each other day to day and week to week:

CREATE TECH-FREE ZONES IN YOUR ROUTINES. For example:

- No phones or screens at the dinner table. Even when it's brief, mealtime can be a time to talk and to connect over the shared ritual of cooking and eating.

- No wi-fi after a certain hour at night. Maybe you'll decide to preserve bedtime as a time to talk, listen, or read together.

STRENGTHEN YOUR HABITS OF PAYING ATTENTION by using some of the active listening techniques you saw in chapter 7. Repeat back what you heard your child say, and comment on it. Ask questions.

USE PHYSICAL ACTIVITY TO BRING YOURSELF BACK INTO YOUR BODY, where your senses are alive to what's going on with your child. Something simple like walking the dog together—or just walking around the block—can get you moving, and become a regular occasion for being present with your son or daughter, and for talking. Go without your phones.

CREATE RITUALS FOR ONE-ON-ONE TIME, AND BE FAITHFUL TO THEM. I often suggest that dads do "rounds" at home, making sure to check in with each child when he gets home from work, or in the evening after dinner. Routines, like setting up a schedule for Dad to read to the kids at bedtime, say, twice a week and for Mom to read on the other nights, create regular presence. One of my friends has three children, and he bonds with them on periodic kids' weekends, during which he'll go away with one child and let the child set the agenda, whether it involves camping, a trip to Disneyland, or a day of swimming and snacking at the beach.

DON'T BE AFRAID OF "FORCED CONNECTION," occasions when you require your children's attendance and participation, even when they (and maybe you) might not ordinarily choose to be there. Presence and connection are skills that require practice. If you've ever tried to meditate and bring your mind back to the present moment, you know how impossible that can seem at first. You learn by "putting your tush on the cushion" again and again—just doing it—even when you're not in the mood. In the same way, you teach your kids to be present for important and new experiences by asking them to be there.

If you give them the opportunity, they'll learn the huge life lesson that they may not be in the mood to be present, but the mood doesn't always know best, and it doesn't get to call the shots. It's inevitable that you'll want to expose your kids to experiences they don't yet value, and you may feel as though you're living in some absurd movie, saying things like, "I know you'd rather stay home with the Xbox, but we're getting in the car now and going to the Grand Canyon!" (Pure torture!)

Yes, you could let your kids' preferences rule because you don't feel like managing their resistance. But I hope you won't. When they try to hunker down in what they know instead of what you'd like them to try, they have no idea what they're about to give up. It's a gift to offer them ways to expand their world with experiences that contrast with the preferences they have today. They may sometimes be navigating the far reaches of their comfort zone, but that's not a bad thing, especially with you at their side.

To be honest, some of the grand opportunities for self-discovery you offer up may look like "dragging them to the relatives"—and that's okay.

When I was a kid growing up, there were many Sunday visits to my grandmother's house. My sister and I would go stir crazy, trying to amuse ourselves while the grown-ups sat in the kitchen speaking Italian—a foreign language to us—because my grandmother spoke little or no English. I resented having to go. Yet those visits were where I got a sense of who my grandmother and big extended Italian family were, even if I only knew the tastes that came out of her kitchen and absorbed the smells and decor of her home. I heard family stories from my aunts and uncles, and saw the array of ways in which the members of our tribe fashioned their lives.

Your kids deserve those kinds of experiences. I am who I am, I know, in part because of those Sundays. If you ask your kids to participate in occasions like this, put aside all your phones and screens, and see what can happen.

CONNECTION THRIVES ON RESPECT

Presence brings you and your children into the same space, paying attention to each other and creating possibilities for connection. What unfolds from there hinges on a second key element: Respect.

The definition you may have gotten from your parents when you were a child could've simply said: Respecting your elders means doing whatever they say without question. Period. But anyone who's gone through adolescence knows how well that works, and how impossible it is for both parent and child to maintain the illusion that parents are infallible and therefore beyond question.

I often notice that if friends my age had strict or tyrannical parents who bludgeoned them by saying "respect me or else," they reject doing that with their own kids. But they don't know how to teach respect instead, so they don't push the issue. I think we all wince when we hear their children—or anyone's kids—speak to the adults in their lives the way they might speak crudely to their peers, calling their fathers stupid or their mothers witches. That's not the path to respect either.

I get the feeling that our understanding of respect has gotten too distorted to be useful, and because respect is the bedrock on which connection is built, I'd like to give you my best sense of what it means between parents and children, how it works best, and how it breaks down.

The dictionary definition of respect that applies here, from the Oxford American Dictionary, is "due regard for the feelings, wishes, rights or traditions of others." It's useful, because it lets us start from the premise that each person—parent or child—has feelings, wishes, and rights that must be honored. I think we can all agree that children have the right to be cared for, protected, and nurtured in an environment that's free of any kind of abuse. They come into the world unable to survive on their own, and need every bit of their imperfect, and very human, parents' wisdom, humor, and love to learn to thrive.

We know our kids are vulnerable, and that we need to protect them. But it can be harder to see them as individuals with feelings and preferences that deserve to be taken seriously. As we look at the facets of respect below, you'll see it flowing both ways—from child to parent, as tradition has always had it, but also from parent to child. If I emphasize that aspect of the flow, from you to your kids, it's because that's what you most clearly control, and what sets the tone for what your children learn and return to you.

TO RESPECT YOUR CHILDREN IS TO LET THEM KNOW THAT YOUR LOVE FOR THEM IS UNCONDITIONAL, that they deserve love simply for being who they are, and don't have to earn it by pleasing you, or anyone else. That means, whether they gets all As or struggle to get even a C, your love will be there. And whether they become the football stars you always wanted or turn out to be kids who prefer to live in their minds, your love is a constant. They should be able to trust that achievement will never be a condition of acceptance, and know that while you may express disappointment or anger or frustration with them, you don't love them less.

As long as your children know you are there for them, no matter what, everything you put on top of that is just circumstance. Your children will be hurt, they'll be denied, have their hearts broken, and struggle. They may run into trouble with drugs or alcohol. Life will happen. But if they are loved unconditionally, they will know they are valued and valuable. They'll contain the core of resilience that will help them cope.

TO RESPECT YOUR CHILDREN IS TO BE THEIR PARENT, NOT THEIR FRIEND. It's common to hear a mother say, "My daughter is my best friend," or for a parent to mention that, "I'm closer to my kids now than to my own friends." But the line between parent and friend is clear, and it's important to keep it in place. Your child—especially when he or she is young and dependent—is *not* your friend, a neutral adult peer with whom you can talk about your marriage, your disappointments with your children, your angers, or your worries. The child's job is to learn to navigate life with your help. It's not to carry the burden of your negative feelings, especially toward a spouse or family members. It's not your kids' job to comfort you or to take on the job of a friend.

The more you treat your children as peers, even though you and they may think it's a sign of respect and honor, the more you're stealing their childhood, their confidence, and their freedom. Psychologists tell us that if you draw kids into your problems, they feel responsible for fixing your distress, and the fact is, they can't. They will fail, and feel both incompetent and guilty for being unable to do the impossible. If you truly respect and honor them, you will seek adult help for your adult problems, clean up messes you make, and keep from drawing them into conflicts you have with other people. It's natural to reach for the ones you're closest to in times of need, but respecting your children means allowing them to *be* children, and handling your adult problems yourself.

At the same time, you have to step up and *be the parent*, the one who takes responsibility for setting expectations, instilling values, and creating safety and structure in the family. I'll talk in more detail about this in the section on safety below, but the point I'd like to make here is this: Your kids depend on you to teach them everything. You're their primal model of how adults function in the world, what they do and don't do. Mature as your kids may seem at age eight or thirteen or sixteen, they are children whose personalities and brains are still developing, and whose social skills and ethics are being shaped by their experiences—especially the ones they have with you. The rules of life you teach, the principles you instill, are their baseline. They deserve to be taught as well as you can teach them—*parented*, not just "friended."

Letting your kids know you expect them to honor you and your rules while they are under your roof keeps your role distinct in their eyes, and yours.

TO RESPECT YOUR CHILDREN IS TO HELP THEM FOLLOW THEIR CURIOSITY AND DISCOVER THEIR STRENGTHS BY EXPLORING WHAT ATTRACTS THEM. Yes, you make them wear helmets and keep them out of traffic when they're determined to race their bikes around the yard because they love to go fast. But you let them try, and learn, and fall, instead of saying, "I wouldn't let my kid do that," or "You're bad for wanting to try this."

Obviously, we're not talking about interests that involve harming other people or putting a child in certain danger. It may not even involve physical activities, but rather being open to a child's unexpected interest in a subject like art or science. Respect means being open to letting kids explore what they're drawn to in ways that involve finding and developing their talents.

TO PUT IT ANOTHER WAY, TO RESPECT YOUR CHILDREN IS TO TEACH THEM TO PLAY THEIR OWN GAME, by which I mean to be the best *them* they can be, rather than trying to be like someone else. My friend Kristin Kittelson is a Board Certified Behavior Analyst whose students are mostly kids with special needs. She works hard to understand them when she meets them, sizing up their learning styles, their goals, their likes and dislikes, their communication styles, and even how long they can work without a break. Then she tailors her lessons to them, building their trust and confidence.

I was struck when she told me she spends 70 percent of her classroom time focusing on helping her students understand their own needs so they can connect with themselves and become better learners. If children don't know how to regulate themselves—that is, know what it takes to bring themselves from a scattered state and focus on the work at hand—they can't learn, she told me. (You may see this in yourself in that spacey time before you "come back to Earth" in the morning with a cup of coffee.)

Parents can help children understand how they learn best and what they like, making it easier for them to teach themselves. "There's a lot of power when a child can advocate for themselves,"

Kittelson says, "and know what their needs are and know they're going to safely get them met."

A child who knows he's a kinesthetic learner can learn to say, "I'll get this faster if I can learn it in a hands-on way. Can you help me do that? I can understand the heart better and learn the parts if I build a model of it." A kid who's wild about dinosaurs might thrive if you help her relate her math homework to her curiosity about the size of a Brachiosaurus.

Developing this kind of self-knowledge allows kids (or anyone) to plug into an infinite source of inspiration, which will carry them toward success and satisfaction far more effectively than any kind of motivation. My friend Janice Bussing makes a distinction that I find to be useful and true: Motivation, she says, pushes you because there's a need. *Inspiration propels you because there's a desire.*

Self-knowledge also helps children keep from panicking when they're faced with situations that operate in ways that seem to put them at a disadvantage.

I saw a great example of how this works, carried into the adult world, when I watched the 2014 Stanley Cup Playoffs, where my team, the L.A. Kings, won multiple games after being down by three goals. Asked how they kept coming back, the coach said, "When we're down, our direction is to find our game, not the goal." By which he meant, the team didn't freak out, get reactive, and try every long-shot plan it could to score a goal. The players kept trusting their proven strengths and strategies, rather than pretending they could suddenly morph into a different sort of goal-scoring machine. As they did that, the coach said, the goals—and the championship—just came.

The invaluable lesson you teach kids by respecting who they are, and helping them find and play to their strengths, is that they'll thrive most easily in life if they work to be the best version of themselves, instead of struggling to become something they're not.

TO RESPECT YOUR CHILDREN IS TO HELP THEM EXPLORE THEIR AUTHENTIC CALLINGS—UNBURDENED BY *YOUR* FEAR. Life has a way of delivering ironies and surprises, and your child's passions and strengths may be the opposite of your own. If you're security-minded, your first response when your son tells you he wants be an artist might be to say, "How in the hell will you make a living?" and try to squelch any more talk about that painting nonsense. But such responses are almost always fear-based. The fear is not that the child should not be the artist he is, but that the child may become the stereotypical *starving* artist.

That fear—*your* fear—can easily derail the work you've done to help the child connect with the passions that will fuel his or her happiness and success.

As your kids explore the world of work, I recommend trusting their passion enough to set your fear aside so they can investigate the possibilities for connecting with what they think they want, then see if they want to proceed.

Your artist child might test the waters by taking classes, talking to people working in the arts, and meeting people you know who make art while working full-time at other jobs. This approach is useful no matter what sort of career or vocation your child feels fired up about. If she wants to be a lawyer, I'd highly recommend that she try to get an internship at a law firm even before heading to law school. The average law school graduate practices less than two years and then drops out of the profession, a potent message about how even solid-sounding dreams can be significantly less appealing in reality.

If your kids want to pursue their dreams after investigating, put aside your fears one more time and help them.

TO RESPECT YOUR CHILDREN IS TO ALLOW THEM TO WEATHER THEIR DISAPPOINTMENTS WITHOUT RESCUING THEM. Of course you want to protect your child from hurt or distress. But as children grow, you do them no service by repeatedly swooping in to save them, distract them, buy their way out of heartbreak or loss, or pull strings to change the outcomes they've earned. Rescuing them weakens their confidence in their ability to rebound and learn for themselves. And I find that it often creates a sort of false confidence that quickly crumbles when they realize that the world doesn't operate on the "Dad will bail me out" principle. When rough patches arrive, it's great to stay connected and offer support, give advice when it's asked for, and remind your children of their strengths and how to maximize them. Then offer love and be a safe home base as they pick themselves up and try again.

It makes sense to keep an eye on your own feelings and fears any time you feel tempted to "save" your child from struggle or failure. Ask yourself: Are you trying to fix the situation because it's harmful to the child, or because *you* feel uncomfortable when your child's path isn't perfectly smooth? (The example in chapter 3 walks parents Maria and Tom step-by-step through this kind of discomfort, and is full of questions that will help you see your emotions and assumptions more clearly.)

TO RESPECT YOUR CHILDREN IS TO SHIELD THEM FROM THE HEIGHTENED EMOTIONS OF A DIVORCE. I know it can be tough to keep adult/child boundaries in place when divorce enters the picture. In contentious divorces, I've often seen parents drag their kids into the pool of disrespect they have for each other. Children suffer when they're asked to take sides, or show support for the parent they're with by listening to blaming, shaming criticism they can't understand. No matter how angry you are at an ex, or how justified you feel you are in your rage, respecting your children requires shielding them from your bitterness and fury.

They don't know how to process or react to criticisms like, "Your mother is a leech and she's trying to punish me," or "Your father could get you anything you wanted, but he's trying to make life tough for us." It's helpful to vent to a friend or counselor, but don't inflict venom on your kids—it poisons them and their future relationships.

A little girl's first love affair is with Daddy, who shows her how a man's behavior makes it safe in a good relationship and in a family. Men get their first understanding of the power and mystery of the feminine from Mom. That's something I wish everyone in a bitter divorce could take to heart: Your children are registering all of what they see you do, and turning it into their model of how the world of men and women works. Let them see the best side of you.

One blind spot I see in divorcing friends is especially painful to witness. When kids resemble a particular parent, they may become targets for projected feelings. A mother might say, "Your brother is just like your father"—in this case *not* a flattering comparison—not only taking out her hostilities on her child, but also making him a target of his siblings. I've also seen fathers become highly critical of their daughters after a separation, and sometimes I want to step in and say, "Cool it. She's not your ex-wife."

For the sake of your kids, I hope you'll check in with friends to be sure you're not doing that, and consciously work to respect and connect with your child as the unique, innocent individual he or she is. Don't hesitate to get help or a clear-eyed perspective from a counselor.

Connection Thrives on Safety, and Structure Creates That for Kids (and Everyone Else)

Connection flows from the feeling that we can be honest about who we are—and therefore vulnerable—without fear. In the last chapter, you saw how establishing ground rules and expectations for behavior in difficult adult conversations helps create a feeling of safety. In the same way, if you create a consistent structure of values, expectations, and accountability that's grounded in respect, you give children the sense of safety that allows them to forge deep connections with you, themselves, and others. Kids are learning this from the bottom up.

Your values tell your children: "This is who we are as people, and a family. These are the standards we hold ourselves to. You'll carry this connection to your family's strengths inside you, and from that unshakeable foundation, you can become anything you want to be."

So let me ask you: What do you want your children to value? What basic principles do you want them to use as a map and compass through life? Your values may come from your religion or reflect wisdom that's been passed to you through your heritage.

Maybe you model your values on what worked in the family you come from or perhaps you reject all that and have come to your own guiding philosophy. What's important is that you and your partner decide what belongs on your list, and stay aligned and consistent on those fundamentals.

A list like this will often contain familiar elements like:

- Do your best.

- Keep your promises; do what you say you're going to do.

- Tell the truth.

- Treat other people as you'd like to be treated.

- Do what you love.

- Don't start something you're not going to finish.

- Leave things better than you found them.

But you may truly value only some of those, or want to emphasize something unique to you. For instance, my list includes something I am constantly asking myself (and my clients): *Can you give what you want to receive?* For me, that question is a way of staying in touch with a sense of appreciation and setting high expectations for myself—two ways of being I value highly. "Can you give what you want to receive?" could be a way into a conversation with a child about the hours and love it took to knit a sweater she received as a gift, and before that to gather the wool, raise the sheep, tend the grass—not to mention the time and energy someone put in to earn money for the sweater, go looking for it, and wrap it up. This line of thinking is an opportunity to suggest that all that goes into creating and bringing us the amazing things we want and receive. It lets us know what it takes to create amazing things ourselves— and primes us to do it.

Seeing that question on my list reminds and inspires me to be my best self. That's what you want the list to do.

You animate that list when you translate your guiding principles into family rules and routines that spell out how you'll put your values into action and help your kids learn what they mean.

What, concretely, does it mean to "treat other people the way you want them to treat you?" In your family, you might spell it out specifically with rules like: "No hitting," or "We always say please and thank you," or "Never disrespect either parent by talking back," or "Ask if anyone is still hungry before you take the last piece of chicken."

"Leave things better than you found them" might produce rules like, "We all keep our rooms clean and don't leave a mess behind us" or "We throw away trash in cans instead of dropping it on the ground."

When values are clear, rules don't feel arbitrary, because the "why" is clear.

As you create this structure of values and expectations, you're building a framework for your children's world, inner and outer, which they'll come to understand the same way they learn anything else—by trial and error, and testing. So it makes sense to have a plan for how you'll handle the tests.

YOU DON'T HAVE TO SAY "YES"
TO PROVE YOUR LOVE

I think it's pretty common to believe—or hope—that the fastest way to show your love for your children is to say yes to them. But nurturing respect, authenticity, and connection is a far greater gift. And often that can involve saying "no": No because what you want doesn't fit with our values. No because we haven't done the work to fund it yet. No because that's the consequence of breaking our rules.

A tear running down your beautiful little girl's cheek or an angry teen's glare can make it hard to stick to your guns, and children know that. Some parents would say their kids can work them better than anyone else. But saying no, even in the face of your child's pleas, manipulations, and heartfelt disappointment, can be the most loving thing you can do for them, especially when a no supports the structures you've built to create safety in your family.

Parents won't always agree, and that's no disaster. I've seen kids learn a lot when one parent says yes to something and the other says no, and they're left to plead their case to both. They sometimes come up with alternate scenarios to try to get more of what they want, and the discussion can create a dialog of "Mom sees it like this, Dad sees it like this, and maybe I can split the difference." It helps kids get clear about why they want what they want.

I've seen children talk themselves out of things when a parent asks, "Why do you want it? What's so special about it? If you really want it, take the money you have saved in your bank." It's interesting to see the kids reevaluate the whole matter. They stop to think and finally say, "Well, I don't know." And they walk away. Sometimes all they really wanted was a voice and a sense of choice, and they were testing their parents—all of which are positive. When parents engage with them, it can show them that they're being listened to, and that they can help create the outcome. The connection that comes from that can be more valuable and memorable than any toy or outing they thought they wanted.

If you're struggling, look back at the material in chapters 2 and 3 on the authentic use of yes and no. The more your children experience that you mean what you say, and say what you mean, the more they'll learn they can trust you—and feel the deep sense of security that trust creates.

THE GREAT GIFT OF ACCOUNTABILITY

A closely related builder of trust and safety is accountability. It's not a popular word these days because people seem to think that to hold someone accountable for particular actions is to judge, blame, and even shame them for their shortfalls and shortcomings. It's as though they see a critical boss poking a finger at an employee's chest and saying, "You made this mess and I'm holding you accountable."

But that's a limited view of a much more generous concept.

Accountability is one of the greatest gifts you can teach a child—it just doesn't come in a pretty blue box.

Accountability, as I see it, is a system of mutual promises that weave relationships together. It's a way of saying, "You can count on me [to do these things], and I can count on you [to do other things]." There's give and take in this system that allows a relationship to thrive when each person does his or her part, and can trust that other people will do the same. This is one of the reasons I believe team sports can be a perfect blueprint for teaching kids accountability and can help them learn about sharing what they have to give regardless of their skill and ability.

As a parent, you can explain the idea of "You can count on me" by letting your kids know they can count on *you* to be sure they have a comfortable home and good food to eat, to love and take care of them every day, to help them learn, and so much more. Because one mom I know does her part in the family, there are clean school clothes in the morning, extra vacations funded by the money she makes as a teacher, stories about lightning on stormy days, secret jokes, home-cooked dinners, and help with music lessons. Almost any parent can come up with an equally wide-ranging list, and share it with their kids. Children are quick to see the gift of what their parents do for them in conversations about accountability. And why wouldn't a kid who recognizes the gifts that flow from "You can count on me" want to be part of that?

The big idea of accountability in this context is: *We are a family and we do things for each other. We can count on each other to do our jobs.* It's not a trade ("After all I've done for you, you little ingrate, you can at least pick up your socks."), it's a symbiotic relationship where everybody shares responsibility for the greater good of the family.

So now it's the kids' turn. What can the family count on each child to do, not just for themselves, but for the family? Some of the things that come up will be intangibles, some quite concrete: Because your daughter does her job in the family, and gives her gifts, there are handmade Christmas decorations, the dog gets walked twice a day, everyone knows science facts because she talks about them at meals, Mom gets a hand with dinner on Fridays, and there's always singing around the house. A list like this should have a balance of appreciation and expectation.

In whatever structure of chores or expectations you create— "It's your job to put a new drawing on the refrigerator every week." "You can be the one who folds the socks and puts them in the drawers." "You and your brother practice music for a half hour every school night."—teach the importance of integrity: Your contributions are important, and we count on them. We know we can count on them, because you do what you say you will do.

Life is hectic and challenging, and neither kids nor adults will always be able to deliver on their promises or meet all of their expectations. But I encourage you to hold the line for accountability and make it mean something by not overlooking it when it's violated, either by you or by the child.

That takes communication, especially when you're teaching young children. Ask:

– Why didn't the promised action happen?

– What went wrong?

– How can we keep it from happening again?

Keep the discussion focused on the issue, not the basic lovability of the child.

Will there be consequences for letting down the family by not delivering on a promise? Will you suspend a valued privilege? If you're going to set consequences, follow through. "No cell phone for the rest of the week" means just that. Your children may not like it, but they will feel safe, knowing that you keep your word, as you expect them to.

When the breakdown is yours, take responsibility and repair your children's trust. There's no way to be a perfect parent. You'll miss a ballgame you promised to attend, snap at your child when you're tired, or lob a hurtful criticism. And your responsibility when this happens is to apologize, reassure the child that he or she is not responsible for what happened, soothe the hurt, and to hold yourself accountable for keeping your promise that it won't happen again. Get support from your partner or another adult if you need it. Connection can't happen without trust.

STRUCTURE ISN'T A PRISON

Putting structure in place for your kids isn't about controlling them, or building a prison of demands. It's one of the ways you make your home more loving. Kids complain about having to clean their rooms or limit their screen time or save up for things they want, but they like direction, and inevitably, they begin to experience the freedom that comes with clear expectations and structures they can rely on. They don't have to keep guessing about what's allowed, or spend their energy trying to figure out what will please or tick off the most powerful people in their lives—their parents. They can use their imaginations to play and create and invent who they want to become, activities that will keep them in close touch with their authentic selves.

Imagination creates something new; it creates change. And kids gain tremendous power from experiencing change from the perspective of excitement and invention, rather than fear. It may look as though they're "just playing" as they turn a cardboard box into a fort or a vehicle for sliding down the lawn. But they're also finding out that they can drive and enjoy change, an attitude that will give them huge advantages in life. That's one of the most empowering lessons that can come from making it safe for them to act like the children they are.

A FEW TIPS FOR IMPLEMENTING CHANGE

The kind of family connection I'm proposing in this chapter isn't easy—especially when it's so automatic for everyone to disappear into their cellphones, games, and tablets that we're used to being alone together instead of making contact. But giving children an environment that supports real connection, and teaches them what connection looks and feels like, is life-changing for them. And for you.

You may feel overwhelmed at the prospect of repairing the connections with your family. It's possible that you're scratching your head and saying, "All this sounds good, but it's opposite of what I've been doing. Where do I start?"

I know change can seem extremely challenging (the reason so many people don't attempt it), but it's approachable if you take it a step at a time.

- First, think about what's important to you. What values do you want your children to have? How do want to adjust the kind of respect you give your child? What expectations do you have of your family members? What points lit up for you in the material above?

- Discuss these things with your spouse and come to an agreement about what you'd like to do. It's not an ordeal—you can go out to brunch with your partner and talk about the values you want your kids to have.

- Start small and build. You don't have to change everything at once. For example, choose one aspect of presence and bring it into your home. Or look through the material on respect and choose one element to focus on this week.

- Inform your family of the changes you want to make. Say, "This is the way things have been, and this is the way I want things to be. This is what we're going to do moving forward." Then slowly implement change, and explain why.

- Teach with your actions. Demonstrate the values you're trying to impart. Stress your own accountability. Get feedback from friends about whether you're stepping into the role of friend, not parent, with your kids.

- Stay the course. As I said earlier, don't make false threats. And don't implement something you're not going to follow up on.

- Adjust as you need to, and enjoy the new level of connection these changes bring into your family.

CHAPTER 9

Connecting to Spirituality

The word "open" has been a steady drumbeat in these pages. I've asked you to stay open to the possibilities that arise when your path isn't blocked by fear. I've suggested listening and observing and questioning your assumptions to open new pathways forward in your business and personal relationships. Opening your mind in that way is like unclenching a fist, and stretching a hand toward other people to make contact and connect.

In this chapter, I'd like to focus on one last facet of openness—the power of an open heart to strengthen your relationship with your spirituality.

I think we all experience moments when it feels as though the familiar world of routines and habits and assumptions about "the way life is" dissolves. We witness the birth of a child. Marvel as we stand on the rim of the Grand Canyon, feeling its immensity. We fall in love and ache for the other person. Feel the spirit of a friend who's battling an illness. And suddenly we're pulled into this moment, without our usual filters of expectation and judgment, without being lured to past or future. We move past the surface of ordinary life, entering something larger.

Heart wide open, we can feel life's urgency and its beauty, and we experience it with a kind of awe that expands us past our minds and into our spirits. We're present to the vastness of life that many people connect with God.

In a major 2008 survey by a group called the Pew Forum on Religion & Public Life, an overwhelming majority of Americans—92 percent—said they believed in God. What we each mean by that is as individual as we are—some people see God as an impersonal, universal spirit, while others embrace a personal God with whom they can have a relationship. People who call themselves nonbelievers or "not religious" often value life itself, or the elegant complexity and beauty of nature.

I can't know exactly how you experience the sense of what's larger than all of us—the endless sky that stretches behind the individual "stars" of our lives. But because I see connection to our spiritual lives as one of our most significant sources of inspiration and guidance, I'd like to end this book by sharing what I've learned about strengthening the sometimes-challenging relationship to spirituality.

When I talk about spirituality, I'm thinking about the practices and beliefs that make the heart receptive to wisdom that's greater than what the mind can know, and that many of us would say connect us with God. I experience my spirituality in the context of religion—I'm a practicing Catholic, but not a dogmatic one, and I've had many struggles over the years with the "right" way to be part of my church.

Because the blocks to spirituality I've worked through are common ones, I'll be talking about some of them here. When I share particulars of my spiritual life, my intention is to use them as case study in how this kind of connection can ebb and flow, strengthen and weaken. The particulars of your experience may well be far different from mine, but I think most of us share the same challenges as we keep refining the shape spirituality takes in our lives.

I've shared the practices of friends from many different traditions, and found beauty and meaning in bar mitzvahs, drum circles, meditations, and tent revivals. My fundamental belief is that there are lots of routes upstairs—many paths to God, which I think of as the all-encompassing force of love. All of life is full of opportunities to move toward that love. If we're willing to listen and keep steering toward what's true for us, we amplify the connection. It's not quite the way they put it in church, but that's what I think spirituality helps us do: Listen, steer, and amplify the presence of love (or God or a higher power, whatever shape that takes) in our lives.

What I learned from
trying to be a good Catholic

I became a Catholic by default—my Italian family has always been Catholic, and the rituals of the church have always been and will always be a foundational part of my life. It's been that way since I was baptized as an infant.

I won't say religion was crammed down my throat, but church, Communion, and Confession weren't optional. I went to Catholic school until junior high, became an altar boy, did time in Catechism class. I absorbed some solid life principles from the Bible stories I liked, the Golden Rule, and the Ten Commandments. But well into adulthood I had a conflicted relationship with religion. I struggled with questions of how to understand God when I kept seeing bad things happen to good and innocent people, and church didn't always seem like a welcoming place for that discussion.

I remember how much it stung, how dismissed I felt, when a priest told me, "There are a lot of things you will never understand that are not for you to understand."

There was definitely some truth in what he said but honestly it left me more frustrated.

I vented about that comment in a confessional a week or two later, and wondered aloud if I really wanted to be in a place that sort of left me at a dead end. Surely God could handle questions, and help me come to terms with them.

The invisible figure on the other side of the partition in the confessional listened, then said, "David, don't ever let any church get in the way of your connection to God."

It was one of the most profound lessons I've ever learned.

I've kept those wise words close as I've continued my search for deeper understanding. I've drawn on them, too, as I've watched the Catholic Church face horrific scandals and atrocities in which deeply broken people and institutions abused their power and shattered the sacred trust of many, especially the child victims of priests. Like all of us, I felt shocked, angry, and betrayed, and deeply concerned about the damage that had been done to the children and to the integrity of the church.

I looked into myself for clarity about what to do next. Many people, their trust demolished, decided to leave the church. But my mind kept returning to the thought that the Catholic Church as a whole feeds, clothes, and houses more people than any other organization in the world. So I kept asking myself: Does the good done by the church as a whole outweigh the bad? Is there something I can do to help correct the damage and be sure this doesn't happen again?

I think everyone who has to ask such questions after a betrayal like this must struggle toward his or her own answers. I decided that rather than leaving, I'd stay in my broken church and remain open to trying to rebuild it, because as destructive as I thought the scandal had been, I believe that the world is much better for having the church at its best, rather than being without it. And the church would be better filled with humbled, galvanized people determined to make it stronger.

I was predisposed to try, because in every kind of relationship, crises come. I'm constantly surprised at how much growth has come into my life from staying open to finding a way forward through a shock, mess, or disappointment, learning what it has to teach me.

The first impulse, I know from my experience, is to close down and head for the door. But in many cases, it's possible to sustain the relationship, on new terms, with new clarity. I was glad that in my own situation, the good I could see outweighed the bad. The unhappy truth is that we've seen many priests and pastors and religious leaders of all kinds fall in sex and financial scandals in recent years. But I think we always have the choice to reach past the crisis and the crap people create and ask if the spiritual mission is worth sustaining. "What's the lesson here?" can be a deeply spiritual question.

THE "RIGHT" WAY TO CONNECT WITH YOUR SPIRITUAL TRADITION MIGHT NOT BE YOUR WAY

It seems almost ironic to me that I searched for reasons to sustain my relationship to my church, because I've had ongoing problems with formal religion. I'm a guy who was born not liking rules, and my church, perhaps like yours, is full of them.

Church is a form of family, though, and for me, because my own family lives three thousand miles away, it's long been my home away from home. At times, that's what's kept me going to services when the kneeling and praying fell short.

To be honest, I went to services for many years with only a few, rare glimpses of God. Sometimes I wasn't quite sure why I was there, always looking for some kind of connection that I couldn't seem to get. But finally—by accident—I found what worked for me and drew me in. It was a music-filled Mass at a church called Saint Monica's, where a twenty-five-member chorus supported by a ten-piece band often sang the prayers. Music has always been my refuge, the one thing that can always soothe me, inspire me, and connect me with my feelings, even my soul. Yet somehow, I hadn't thought of it as something that could carry me toward God.

There was a moment in this service, though, when everyone was asked to hold hands and the choir's cantor began singing a call-and-response version of the Lord's Prayer, which is simultaneously one of the central prayers in Christianity and one that is often said in rushed, rote fashion because it's so familiar. The beauty of this version, which is called the "Echo Our Father," pierced me. It was as though someone had reached into my chest, pulled it open, and filled me up with something so big, it had to be God. I got tingly from head to toe, and I felt changed, redefined somehow. In those years, it would've taken an act of Congress to make me shed a tear, but it was all I could do to keep from crying. I had found my connection, and my congregation, and I was hungry for more.

That powerful moment made my spirituality real in a way it hadn't been before—which is not to say it got easier. Even in the midst of this musical, welcoming place, I was still me, and I brought with me all my old doubts. Yep. Everywhere you go, there you are.

I continued to struggle with my longtime question—"Should I be here?"—every time I found myself distracted by a pretty girl in a tight dress as I waited for Communion. I knew that God was the last thing on my mind, and I didn't feel good about it. I wondered if I was feeling what I was supposed to feel when I prayed. Was I just going through the motions if I listened to the cantor now, or recited prayers with no electricity or epiphany? Was I supposed to feel God right there somehow? And if I didn't, did that mean I wasn't trying hard enough, or just didn't belong?

I realized that, more than ever, all those questions had to do with me, not the church I was standing in.

I found my way through that thicket of doubts, though. And it happened on a hiking trail. As I walked alone, my mind calmed down. I felt connected to myself, and, very quietly, to my spirit and to God, in ways I had been unable to in church. As I've mentioned that to people over time, I've realized how many of us have problems with the formalities of religion, and how nature can be the temple that brings us face to face with the divine. It seems fitting to look for the source of life and light in the glow of a sun-drenched day or while losing ourselves in the Milky Way. Some people can concentrate on the services at church and get the inspiration they need, but my mind is so busy that I feel the most peaceful in nature, where there's much less human distraction.

Once I realized that I could go hang out with God in the quiet of my hikes—Matthew Kelly calls it "spending time in the classroom of silence"—it was easier to be in my church, and enjoy the love and joy that I get from the people with whom I share the Mass. That connection has always been a huge part of my spiritual life, and now I could enjoy it fully because I didn't have the feeling that in the midst of it, I would fail to connect to God. I saw that some of that connection would always come to me when I was alone in nature, and I'd experience some in community. The different flavors of my spirituality could feed each other. And no one was saying it had to be either/or.

I've come to realize that if I can still my mind enough, there is always something meaningful for me in the services. Now I approach church the same way I do my time outside: I go without expectations, listening with a mind that's as quiet as I can make it, and staying open to whatever comes. One week, the message I need to hear might be in a story from a scripture that seems to speak directly to my life, or a line of a hymn or prayer that I never noticed before. Another week it might be a story from one of our many great priests or a homily from our monsignor. It could be a passing comment from someone less fortunate passing through our parking lot. And sometimes—often, actually—it's a passage of music or someone's transcendent singing that reaches inside me. I may not find what I think I'm coming for, but there's always a spiritual connection available.

What made it possible for me to embrace religion wasn't saying "church bad/nature good," but coming to my authentic self, and honoring the way I most naturally connect with my spiritual side when I put expectations aside and breathe into the present.

In this arena of life, as with all others, the same principle applies: Following your authentic leanings, rather than what you "should" feel or do, creates the most powerful connections.

A FEW WORDS ABOUT FAITH

Many of my friends and clients struggle with spirituality. It's easy to question our faith in ourselves and in what we cannot see. But I think faith connects us to the miraculous, which is the often-invisible backdrop of ongoing good in our lives.

Wayne Dyer tells a story about talking with a brain surgeon who says he has huge doubts about many things he can't see, and Dyer says (I'm paraphrasing), "You've cut open a lot of brains. Did you ever see love or imagination in the brain?" You can't see or touch those things. Your heart can ache with longing for someone you love, yet that love isn't something you can find in open-heart surgery.

The mystery of God's love is only one hurdle to faith, of course. There's also the question I had as a young man about why bad things happen to good people, and why a God I understood as absolute Love would allow that. We all have our own answers—the challenge and journey of spirituality, the mysteries of faith and feeling your way toward what you genuinely believe isn't easy. But I will say that the God I have made peace with doesn't want a codependent relationship with me. I understand the love flowing my way as unconditional, not the result of any kind of bargaining I do. And as I navigate the ups and downs of my life, I work to make the love I send back to God equally free of deals and bargaining. Even when bad things happen, my faith says that my life, and all life, is better with love and gratitude and the question "What's the lesson in this for us?"

TRY IT YOURSELF: SOME QUESTIONS TO SPARK POSSIBILITIES FOR CONNECTION

1. What obstacles are getting in the way of your connection to God or your spirituality?

2. What one step can you take toward making contact again?

3. How can you experience your spiritual side/God and simply show up with the intention of being fully present to what's happening in the moment?

4. What do you know pulls you out of your mind and into your larger spirit? How can you spend more time doing it?

5. If you've lost your faith, to what extent have you tried to find it? Compare that to the effort you'd exert and pain you might endure if you misplaced a check for $50,000.

6. In terms of spirituality, what do you believe?

CHOOSE CONNECTION

YOUR SPIRITUALITY WILL
FIND YOU IF YOU LET IT

We all have a relationship to spirituality, whether we have a relationship to God or not. Even having no practice or regular contact with your spiritual side is a kind of relationship.

I believe that if you make yourself available, your spirituality will
find you, choose you. If you've been out of touch with your own
spiritual side and miss it, you can reestablish a connection by taking
just one step toward your spirituality. You can make that mean anything you want it to mean, and start any time. You can begin with
a prayer, a walk in nature, or even just a thought.

You might want to try this simple, personal practice: Stop once
a day to take a few slow, deep breaths and sit quietly, holding the
thought, "I'm here." The words are a way of reminding yourself
that you are present, right now. They're also an announcement,
and invitation, to whatever your spirit wants to bring you. Sit,
breathe, and listen. How long? You'll know. Try showing up in this
way for a week and see what happens. Let it be your experiment in
reconnecting to your spirituality, even a few moments at a time. If
you're a walker, walk. If nature speaks to you, go out and listen.
But announce yourself. Say, "I'm here."

If you're trying to help children connect to a spiritual tradition,
remember that they'll learn more from your actions than your
words. If you *demonstrate* a religion that offers them love, safety,
and trust, a kind of practice that's full of generosity, and that offers
forgiveness and belief when things go wrong, you won't have to
force-feed them anything. They'll absorb and learn to practice what
you do. But don't expect a child who does not feel safe, loved, and
cared for by parents to believe in a God they can't see. As the old
saying goes, children learn what they live. And the love they experience through you will be their first taste of the larger spirit of
Love.

For all of us, doubts happen. Spiritual relationships are like any
other—they live and breathe, and they aren't always smooth. There
have been many times when I couldn't connect to my spirituality,
couldn't feel its presence as I longed to. But I've learned that those

interruptions are like those that occur in every other part of life. Every belief we have gets tested, no matter what we do, and some days we give up. Those are the days when we just can't understand why bad things happen to us and people all around the world. But I've found that my biggest growth has come in the wake of my biggest challenges, and that includes the ones to my spirituality.

Faced with loss or tragedy, it's easy to lose faith. At those times, I think it's important to ask: What have I lost faith in? Myself? My church? My ability to get the results I want from my beliefs? Often I think that we lose faith when our expectations have not been met, yet it's possible to sustain our spirituality, sometimes by giving the love or hope we want to receive.

Perhaps you know that for part of her life Mother Teresa suffered over not feeling the presence of God. Letters published after her death show her struggling with that absence. "The silence and emptiness is so great that I look and do not see, listen and do not hear," she wrote in 1979. Yet even with that, she wrote of wanting to "love Jesus as he has never been loved before," and it's incredibly moving to me to see the tremendous good that came from love and belief even in the face of what seemed like silence or absence.

HOW TO FORGIVE YOURSELF

Inspired as I am by Mother Teresa and other great spiritual leaders and teachers, it's sometimes hard for me to think of them without measuring myself against them and feeling myself fall short. We come to spirituality in a quest to be better people, but a major block to spiritual connection can be the sense that we're not worthy recipients or practitioners of the teachings that are meant to uplift or transform us.

Sometimes, before we can embrace the promise of unconditional acceptance that so many traditions offer, we first have to forgive ourselves. That kind of forgiveness doesn't mean forgetting what we did, or walking away from our responsibility to apologize and repair the harm we caused to other people.

Forgiveness, to use a definition favored by Oprah Winfrey, means "Giving up the hope that the past could have been any different." It's that impossible longing that allows us to replay and replay our wrongs, sometimes keeping the past more alive than the present, and often binding us to shame, the feeling that we are, for all time, bad. In releasing that feeling, we free ourselves to receive empathy and compassion. And when we can do that, we can finally extend them to others, and take in the compassion of our spiritual teachers.

I've used the forgiveness exercise below to help clients lift the burden of past wrongs.

FORGIVENESS EXERCISE

We can't change the past, but we can change how we hold onto it. These steps can help shift your relationship with the shame of negative past actions:

1. Write down the story of the event or actions for which you seek forgiveness. Be as specific as possible. Be aware of where you feel regret, resentment, or bitterness.

2. Run your story through the questions below. Consider asking a friend or loved one who knows you, and who might be familiar with the situation, to help you. Write down your answers.

3. Why do I need forgiveness now?

4. What am I most sorry for?

5. How will life be different for everyone involved if I can forgive myself?

6. I can't change history, but if I had to do things over, what would I do differently and why?

7. What am I willing to do to make things right, if given the opportunity?

8. Take any direct action you need to make amends. If the party or parties you hurt are no longer alive or are unwilling to accept your effort, write a letter of apology and read it aloud.

9. Write a letter asking yourself for forgiveness and read it aloud. If it would support you to have another person witness your request for forgiveness, ask that person to do so.

10. Reread your description of the event. Feel the negative emotions that are still alive there and make a conscious choice to release them. You are a human who makes mistakes, and you can choose to let go of the pain you feel.

11. In a safe place, burn the description and throw the ashes in the trash outside your house, or wash them down the drain. This is a symbolic break between the past and your new present, a symbol of letting go.

12. Give yourself permission to move forward with the wisdom of your experience, but without the hope that you can change the past.

I believe you will feel a burden lifted after going through this process. I used it with a client who had treated his sick father badly thirty years ago when he was just a kid and who had never forgiven himself. Now, as an adult, he could begin to see that the kid had probably been angry and scared.

As you do this work, you, too, will likely find perspective that helps you step beyond old self-recrimination. If you have an opportunity to speak with the person or persons you wronged, you will have the clarity to ask directly for their forgiveness as well. And if you can't make that direct contact, you can look at yourself in the mirror and say, "I have done all I can, to the best of my ability. I can do no more." My client was liberated by doing this. And I know that his father, who had been long gone to heaven, would be glad his son had finally received the forgiveness he wasn't there to give. Self-forgiveness opens us to love, the force at the center of our spirits.

PRACTICING NON-ATTACHMENT, ESPECIALLY IN LOVE

If there's one thing I'd like to leave you with, it's the knowledge that no matter what path it takes, and no matter the outcome, love itself is vast, and in loving, you'll experience some of your spirit's rich truth. Be open to its surprises.

Love is the great teacher of one of the truths I find most valuable, and life-changing, in my work with connection: More than we know or generally acknowledge, our lives run on faith. For as much as we can do to improve the way we connect with people and master the situations in our lives, we don't control the outcome. Paradoxically, the most genuine growth, success and happiness comes from giving our all—and then giving up any attachment to what happens.

Non-attachment means being authentic to who you are, doing your best, loving with all your heart, and putting expectations aside. In other words, you want something. You're excited at the thought of it happening. You're full of hopes. But you're also open to a whole range of outcomes. You don't resist the possibility that things won't play out in your ideal scenario, or that you'll be offered something different from what you had in mind. You're open to the idea that what you want may not be what's best for you right now, though it may take time to see it. You're open to the growth that comes from difficulty, or other people's preferences. And you're open to surprises that take your breath away.

Most of all, you have faith that the result you create with your authenticity, your effort and your heart will deliver what's most needed, even if it doesn't take the form you expect.

Practicing non-attachment takes work. When things don't go quite the way we want, the tendency is to try to control the outcome or other people's reactions. That's where we get in trouble. It's painful to stand in our vulnerability and feel our way through the discomfort of being challenged or disappointed. That's especially true in love. But as you'll see in the story below, love has a way of expanding us regardless of the circumstances when we let ourselves release our attachment to the form it takes.

THE POWER OF OPENNESS: LOVING LIKE GOD

Years ago, I had a strange experience with a woman that led me to one of my most profound lessons about love, and God.

She was a longtime friend—beautiful, smart, and strong, but with a vulnerable part I had never known before. We were at a party, catching up, as we hadn't seen each other for a while. There were many people around, and lots going on, but we were so tuned in to each other that everything around us seemed to fall away. To this day I have no idea what we were talking about. But I vividly remember that all of a sudden my heart started to pound in a way it never had before. It was so loud even Helen Keller could've heard it. How my friend didn't notice is beyond me. My body— my *heart*—was telling me in no uncertain terms that this was it. This was the woman I'd been waiting for.

In that moment, I didn't know what to do. I had fallen in love before—at least I thought I had—but this felt very different. It wasn't just the groin speaking, or the head. My whole being knew she was the one.

I've often wondered why my heart opened so suddenly to her that day of all days. I left the party to visit my friend Ray, who'd had a long battle with cancer and was in the hospital. As I sat with him, his eyes closed and I realized he had gone to God. I don't know if you've ever witnessed someone's spirit leaving at the moment of death, but I will tell you that I knew right then, if I hadn't known before, that we are much more than our bodies.

I left him with a sense of urgency about life. To be with death is to know how very precious our time here is, and how very brief. When you know that, you want to grab life and love with both hands. You don't want to wait. So I know I was full of emotion, living in the in-between, almost looking at my own life from the perspective of Ray's wise spirit.

When I got home, I called my friend to confirm plans we'd made for the weekend. She thought about it and decided while we were on the phone that while she liked having me in her life, she didn't feel any "chemistry" with me and just wanted to be friends.

I was disappointed, but to be honest, I was still in shock after losing Ray, and I let my mind step up and say her rejection didn't matter right then. I moved on to other relationships, and so did she. We saw each other at occasional social events, and we were always friendly. But I was shocked to realize that my feelings were only getting stronger.

I was still deeply in love with a woman who only wanted to be my friend and nothing more. That's an old story, of course. What surprised me was that I couldn't get past it, even though I wanted to. It didn't make sense to me, especially given the brief time we spent together and the casual kind of interactions we had.

When I tried dating other women, this persistent love was in my way, and it didn't seem to be leaving. I wasn't about to chase her or try to persuade her that she was wrong—that's not my way. Her feelings were her feelings. I don't see any point in trying to make people feel what they don't genuinely feel.

"But what is this really about?" I kept asking myself. And it came to me that this love had to be for a bigger purpose that wasn't clear to me yet. I would have to take it on faith and see where it led. I had all this love and nowhere to go with it. So I did what I always do—I tried to figure it out.

This crazy, frustrated, churning love became something I worked on deeply by myself and with my men's group. Those guys are a core part of my life, and I have done my deepest and best work with them. Finally, after years of hearing about this woman, the group presented me with a demand—put up or shut up.

"David, you have to tell her how you feel," they said.

"Why?" I asked. "What's the point?"

"You're holding onto this energy, and it's for her. It would be good for you to tell her," they said. "Besides, what do you have to lose? You already don't have her."

Good point. I use that philosophy all the time with my clients. But it's easier to give advice than take it, even when you know it's wise.

I pictured the conversation I'd be having with her. Have you ever told somebody you loved them, knowing they didn't have the same feelings for you? It would make me vulnerable in a way I'd never been before. I wasn't happy about it, and yet I'd be doing it by choice.

"Why the hell am I doing this?" I asked myself again and again as I worked up to calling her. But I was convinced that this love had something to give me, and I was going to find out what.

We're told that God never tires of hearing prayers from us, but I think I really tested that theory, because I asked God countless times why I was feeling this way. What was the purpose? I knew there was more to this than being brokenhearted, because I'd been there before. This was different.

Finally, I managed to make the call. I asked her to meet with me. When we were sitting face to face, I did the typical-man thing and beat around the bush for fifteen minutes before I got to the part about my deep love and feelings for her.

She was kind. She listened quietly, and told me she was sorry she didn't feel the same way. I left with my dignity intact.

I'd had no expectations except that I'd probably humiliated myself, but I thought I'd feel better once I stated my truth. The fact is, I didn't, though I was relieved when it was over.

I looked back on the experience, proud of myself for staying open in the face of rejection, something I'd never been able to do before. But I kept feeling I was missing some bigger meaning in what I'd been through. The only thing that I was sure of was that this was about much more than the love I couldn't have.

THE LESSON

On a men's group retreat in the Pacific Northwest, I finally understood the spiritual lesson in my whole irrational saga. I was talking for the 500th time about the frustrating love that wouldn't leave me alone, and for the 500th time I found myself asking, "Why did I have to fall this way for someone who doesn't love me back?"

Paul, one of the guys, looked me right in the eye and said, "Why does there have to be a reason?"

"What do you mean?" I replied. "Of course there's a reason."

He paused, then said, "What if you just love her and that's it?"

208

There was another long pause before I said anything, because I didn't quite get what he meant right away, and some of the other guys didn't either. "What the hell, Paul. What are you talking about?" one of us said.

But all of a sudden I got it, and I could feel the knowing pass through my whole body. He was talking about unconditional love. I had to smile. If that's what unconditional love looks like, I thought, no wonder it's so hard.

"What if you just love her...." It may sound odd to say, but those words gave my love a plan and a purpose, even if it doesn't ever go away. I could understand it in the way I understand how God loves—that love is always there, whether you choose it or not. And whether or not this woman chose me, I could love her without condition, appreciating her, wanting the best for her, and respecting her freedom to seek the love *she* wanted. It's not easy. In fact, it's by far the toughest thing I have ever endured.

But it's shown me the immensity of the love we can have for each other, and how big our hearts can be. To give or experience that kind of love expands us in ways we could never imagine otherwise.

This lesson was so life altering that it was surely from God. It didn't change our relationship on the outside, but it transformed me inside. We can't control what happens, but we can always choose to expand into love.

I know I will always love her no matter the circumstance. I can't control it. And I can say that for once in my life, I have loved like God.

THE POWER OF ACCEPTING
WHERE AND WHO YOU ARE

Love without conditions. I think a lot about what that means. Experiencing what it was like to give love stripped of expectations, I found that I was able to receive it in a different way. I realized that though I had always assumed the Big Love of God was unconditional, I'd actually behaved as though there were endless terms and conditions attached. I divided my life into the "religious, toeing-the-line" part and the "everything else" part—parties, women, beer with the guys—and I only made the "religious" stuff part of my spiritual life. I had the idea that "God wouldn't like it" if I brought the totality of myself into our spiritual relationship. I kept the rest separate, or at least undiscussed, in my spiritual life.

But it finally sunk in that God, as I understand Him, is not keeping score. Unconditional love, as I read it, means we bring everything we are to the "all that is" of God, and trust that it will belong. We're loved and accepted, period. No need for hiding.

It takes a lot of energy to keep a secret, to hide a part of yourself. And it's hard to be in the present moment—the place where we come in contact with our spirituality—when you're pushing away any part of yourself or your situation. When I gave up my habit of hiding and began showing up in my spiritual life as my authentic self, I began to experience a ripple effect of acceptance. Believing I was unconditionally accepted, I could more deeply embrace my authentic self, even the "weird" parts that didn't fit my preconceptions of how I should feel or be. The part, for instance, that felt closer to God while hiking than while sitting in the pews. I could get to know what actually existed in myself, instead of what I wanted to be there.

I began to look around—inside and out—and say, "This is what is. What's my next step?" I could listen for guidance from the truest part of myself, and from God. I've been surprised by the synchronicities that this seems to set in motion. I notice what I'm missing, what I need, where I've fallen short, and I connect much more easily with the ideas and resources that can help.

My life has gotten much simpler. Instead of seeing the trash on the ground in front of my office building and flying into a rage of judgments about the thoughtless jerks who can't even pick up their own lousy coffee cup, I just notice what's there, and I respond by taking the next step: I pick up the trash and throw it away.

This is what is, right here, right now. That's the ground on which we meet ourselves, and find the spiritual connection that can help us navigate whatever comes.

All of us, I think, will face challenges to our expectations not just for relationships, but for the way life will unfold. Despite all we hope, we won't live forever on earth or be free of disappointment and heartache. We'll face some of the worst things we can imagine, along with the greatest joy. Our spirituality can bring us support when we need it, and help give meaning to what otherwise might be incomprehensible. If we can stay openhearted, it will keep us moving, moment by moment, toward love.

Epilogue

In this book, we've followed the trail of connection as it flows from a deep acceptance of the authentic self into a widening world of personal relationships, business dreams, and the realm of spirituality. My hope is that you'll be inspired to keep honoring who you are—and set aside the idea that you have to be anything else—as you build a life that fulfills you. I know authenticity isn't easy, especially in a time when there's intense pressure to crowdsource wisdom, and play to what's popular, or what we think most shines up our image, instead of what's most genuine for us.

You might not always like what you see when you take a close look at your authentic self. The challenge is to accept the "difficult" or "imperfect" parts too. I thought for a long time that if I kept doing my inner work, I could change anything about myself. But I finally realized that there are parts of me that simply aren't going to change. What I can tell you is that there's something almost magical about accepting that, and ending the adversarial relationship with the parts I wish were different. Once I did that, I could free up the lifetime's worth of energy I'd used to resist them. Whether you're an introvert who has tried everything to become extroverted, or a creative type who's shoehorned him/herself into a left-brained corporate box, you can shift course and honor your deepest nature. Once you do, you'll find yourself connecting with people and situations that suit you better, and bring a new ease into your life, a liberating sense of being fully comfortable in your own skin.

I've suggested many techniques and experiments for bringing honesty and depth into your life, and I hope you'll keep trying and using them. As you do, remember to go slowly. Lasting change is gradual. What never works is the "all or nothing" approach, by which I mean deciding to start the revolution and change *everything* in a relationship all at once OR deciding to read and absorb but *not take action.*

Take one small step. And then another. I heard it put best by Deion Sanders, who has said you never really arrive, you're always on your way.

My clients have used the tools and approaches in this book to revive their businesses, set off in completely new career and life directions, breathe passion back into their relationships, and put themselves on the path to what they've always felt they were meant to do. You can too—if you start small, stay honest and open, and keep going.

Bringing your authentic self into your relationships and your business takes great courage. You have to shed your masks and armor and be willing to be hurt. But when you do, you'll find that you've also opened yourself to closeness, energy, inspiration, and joy that weren't there before.

My own life has changed significantly as I've gone more deeply into my exploration of authenticity and connection. I was a tough, lonely kid who thought something was wrong with him because he couldn't connect to much of anything authentic. I think a lot of us have a misfit kid like that inside. This work is dedicated to freeing the adults we all became and to the children who will be the beneficiaries of all our efforts.

My days now are full of people I love, and signs, large and small, that I'm doing exactly what I was meant to in living my purpose. I'm surrounded by love, as well as family, friends, and colleagues who laugh a lot, know me for who I am, and tell me the truth. And every day I notice happy accidents and synchronicities that help me along my path. Today I see God in everything and know for sure only one thing. My faith has saved my life.

That's what connection looks like, and it's what I wish for you. Please drop me a line and let me know what happens as you bring the power of connection into your life.

God Bless You.

David Giuliano
September 2015

Acknowledgments

I am first and foremost grateful to God for always providing everything I needed, whether I liked it or not. Writing this book has truly been a test of my faith in you. There were countless times I asked for guidance and you answered. Saint Monica Catholic Community, which has been my spiritual home and gave me a connection to God I never knew existed, has supported me in ways only God has knowledge of.

My parents, Louis and Nancy Giuliano, led the way in showing me how to serve others. This book is a reflection of all the love that they have given me. My sister (and artist/songwriter) Christine Giuliano inspired me to reach past all my limiting beliefs through her own actions. Thank you also to the Lascoes and the Feldmans, who have been my family here on the West Coast.

My dear friend Philip J. Kavesh shares my passion for all things difficult, in a New Jersey kind of way. His example challenged me to improve and seek ways to make things better, and he helped me pave the road through places I never knew I wanted to go. Of The Men's Group—Paul MacCready, Jon Hocker, Ray Hovick, Rick Mills, Douglas Aaron Nation—there are no words that can fully express how each of them affected my life. This book would not exist if they hadn't encouraged me to live on my edge.

Many people offered their wisdom and guidance over the years as I conceptualized and finally wrote this book. I owe them all a debt of gratitude: Kirsten Kittelson, Christine Porath, Molly Lyda, Daniel Hovee, Sharon Dougan, Nina Boski, Gerard Martorano, Derek Emery, and Karen Brundage.

The Institute for Professional Excellence in Coaching trained me—and thus allowed me to realize my true purpose. Other teachers and authors have inspired and shaped me as well, and I would be remiss if I didn't acknowledge specifically Dr. Wayne W. Dyer *(Wishes Fulfilled)*, Marianne Williamson *(A Return to Love)*, Allison Armstrong, and David Deida.

Finally, editor Donna Frazier Glynn made my thoughts and words come to life on these pages. I am so grateful for her patience and wisdom, which made this book a reality. Thanks as well to copy editor Jennifer Brown, who put the final touches on the manuscript, and Robin Rauzi, who helped me wrap it up and bring it home.

Notes